AF261431

DEALING WITH DIFFICULT PEOPLE FOR SPIRITUAL PEOPLE

USING THE FRICTION OF OUR MOST CHALLENGING RELATIONSHIPS TO CULTIVATE THE PEARL OF HEIGHTENED CONSCIOUSNESS

BETHANY GONYEA

NUMINOUSONLINE.ORG

CONTENTS

DEDICATION

My Darling Daughters

*As I progress through life passages ahead of you, I often wonder
how you will feel when you reach my life stage, and I always
hope you will have an easier passage.*

*To that end, each time I learn something about this life and how
to live it feeling more free and whole, I send the wisdom through
the timelessness of the ethers in the hopes that you will receive it,
benefit from my discoveries, and experience an easier passage
for you and your children.
This book is one of those endeavors.*

*You are my favorite people and always will be.
I love you more than you will ever know.*

Mom

PREPARATION

So you are dealing with a difficult person?

Did you read self-help books to improve your relationship? Have you tried looking within to determine how to clean up your side of the street? Have you performed universal spiritual practices such as prayer, forgiveness, acceptance, and loving-kindness to smooth the relationship? Have these efforts worked?

I didn't think so. I am not surprised.

You would not have purchased this book if those efforts had worked. However, making such efforts to improve your relationship tells me something about your character, so I have both good and bad news for you. The "bad" news is that you have unknowingly been admitted to Spiritual Law School. In other words, you have matured enough to have your butt kicked, whether you want it to be or not! The good news is that the spiritual law curriculum you are about to undergo will make you one awesome spiritual ninja! The formidable challenge you face offers you the unique opportunity to become someone who comprehends your power and worth in any situation and knows how to wield it well. Your current relationship challenge is preparing you to put your real power into skillful service for yourself and others.

You may say, "*If dealing with this difficult person is how I get my spiritual juris doctorate, no thank-you! In fact, I don't remember wanting to apply to spiritual law school. I want to return this book and return to my simple, straightforward life where I can just "be me" and not be so aware.*" If this is how you feel, you could put this book aside; however, chances are, you will continue experiencing even more intensity of the same. Does that work for you? I didn't think so.

You are the type of person who chooses to continue reading this book because you know there is a power in you so strong and steadfast that you reject discouragement and disempowerment as your final destination. This strength within you is what has already made you successful in other parts of your life, but this one relationship makes you question...*everything*. Everything you thought you knew, everything you thought you believed in, and everything that illuminates your map of the world.

Your previous success is precisely what has put you in the prestigious Heightened Consciousness Spiritual Law School admissions line. You are now being called to apply your success skills to evolve into a new version of yourself. The real you. The authentic you. The humble you. The wise you. This problematic person has appeared to help you access your more authentic self, which is more discerning, loving, and enlightened than the old you. In fact, when you eventually work through this challenging relationship and integrate these grandeur aspects of yourself, you may even attribute this complicated person to being your most outstanding teacher in this life time. (I am glad I am not with you now, so you can't throw anything at me!) If this is a difficult concept for you to accept, I invite you to put your hesitations aside and trust in a body of work bigger than all of us.

The information in this book is "bigger than all of us" because it follows fundamental laws of energy distribution within ourselves, between people, and between you and your version of "God." This will not be a book about "he said, she said" stuff. Instead, it will rely on spiritual energetic principles that foster growth and development by reestablishing wholeness. There is a law in nature. Every animal, plant, or person only grows or dies; nothing stays the same. The premise of this book is that the challenging relationship you are experiencing offers you an opportunity to rouse growth within yourself so you can return to your true identity as an infinite spiritual being.

Buddha's teachings have been summarized as saying, "enlightenment is progressive disillusionment." This world must disappoint us before we are willing to trade up into a greater understanding of our true identity. In other words, if the world were all rainbows and roses, we would not be inspired to reach for something more. When we understand the power of spiritual law curriculum, we realize that the parade of challenges in our lives will never stop, but we also embrace that they come to up-level us. We recognize that challenges invite us to stop skating based on prior knowledge and begin remodeling ourselves to become something more exquisite, similar to how a caterpillar emerges from the chrysalis as a beautiful butterfly. We learn to acknowledge that feelings of powerlessness reveal it is time to accept that now is the time to drop all we thought we knew and become teachable again!

If you choose to undergo this curriculum, everything within you will be up for renovation. If you decide not to resist your demolition, you will build on your beautiful remains and reorganize around your invincible nature. You will come to identify with the part of you that water can't get wet and fire can't burn. You will come to rely on your inner nature rather than your outer world. This internal navigation will hold you so well that you will prefer your new inner calibration over old habitual patterns. You will like yourself more and enjoy life as the magical mystery tour it was meant to be.

However, as we reorganize within, there will be a period of "unsettling." Metaphorically, there will be a time when your hand is empty as you release a pint to "reach" for a quart. We instinctively recoil from this emptiness as we desperately cling to the known. Our skills have worked for us in the past, right? So, we don't want to be bothered with new learning. We wish to continue with life as we knew it. We want to refrain from recalibrating to our Infinite Nature. We don't trust it, so ironically, we go "kicking and screaming!" to our most beautiful selves! As we continue on the spiritual path, we are delighted to discover that the emptiness is full of richness and possibilities! We would no longer consider relying on our prior understandings because we would find them stale, artificial, limited, and boring. We understand that in that emptiness is where we commune with a loving intelligence that connects us all; it is also the field from which greater wisdom emerges. Paradoxically, we are invited to be nothing but our whole, infinite, loving selves in the fertile emptiness.

But, I am getting ahead of myself because the pathway to living from your more Infinite nature is hard-earned and often not addressed in current Western pop spirituality circles. We have bleached our spirituality in a similar way to how we bleached our bread and bleached our rice. People in the West often think that spirituality is simply positive Facebook memes. Nothing could be further from the truth! Advanced spirituality is much more gritty. As we follow the spiritual path, our egos get hammered year after year. If we reject depression and do the spiritual work required of us, through these struggles, we learn how to "detach" into delicious freedom. The entire process is counterintuitive. You don't see many Instagram memes on these topics because people's egos want to avoid hearing them. We resist renovation so much that our spirit intuitively draws to us a "difficult person" or "petty tyrant" because they lead us to work on ourselves in a manner we would never explore without them. If we don't use the opportunity to renovate from within, they will continue to annoy and terrorize us with distractions. Even worse, if we ignore the lessons one difficult person offers, we may draw more of them!

Petty tyrants offer us the gifts of helping us to reveal our self-deceptions and eliminate self-importance, all while teaching us to become far more discriminating regarding how we spend our precious life force. There is no cheap grace. This path is an initiation. I won't sugarcoat it. It can be rough. There will be times when it will feel uncomfortable. However, when you know the curriculum and the destination, you can undergo your lessons with pluckiness, knowing that one way or another, you are on your way to feeling lighter and happier. You endure your lessons anticipating knowing you are stretching into greater freedom. The process gets much easier as we progress. We start to embrace challenges because we know we will benefit from them.

Eventually, upon graduating from the Heightened Consciousness Spiritual Law School, we use what we learned from our spiritual law degree to greet difficult people as "friends and equals," knowing they will only enrich our lives.

Are you ready to receive the goodies from the challenge you are facing?

Ok, so let's begin!

HOW TO APPROACH THIS BOOK

You have been forewarned that your status quo is up for complete renovation. In this section, I will share how we will approach your remodeling. Let me begin by adjusting expectations for what this book will and will not offer. First, if you do not consider yourself a spiritual person, the map of the world I refer to may not be an orientation you are familiar with or honor, so it is not worth wasting your time or money on this book. Feel free to return it. I will accept it back gladly.

For spiritual people, I will make generalizations regarding a spiritual way of life you may not embrace. We are all on different spiritual journeys, and no two of them ever, probably in the history of time, have ever been the same. You do you! I must make certain generalized assumptions regarding spiritual orientations to write this book. You may have never studied at such depths or have different religious views, or maybe you are just returning to the concept of God or Source Energy after abandoning it for years due to religious abuse. Whatever your orientation, please mute mental pontifications regarding assumptions I am making about the audience of this book if they get in your way of the general discussion. Try to set your intention toward obtaining insights from the text that will help you despite these resistances. For instance, I will try not to use the word God because it seems to make many people do mental summersaults, not in a good way. My goal is to use the name Source Energy; however, if the word God is mentioned, go with whatever "God" means to you.

Next, please accept that you will **not** learn from this book how to "fix" your petty tyrant or even how to deal with your difficult person in ten easy steps. The most powerful lessons of this book will not be transferred through words. Your greatest lessons will be revealed while learning to calibrate to your Higher Self while performing the five explorative meditations accompanying this text. In the mind-body-spirit explorations, I lead you to calibrate yourself to your soul and your spirit first -- before attempting to transform your relationship with your "difficult person."

You will progress little if you stay in your head with the intellectual information offered. You would only gain mental insights into your situation. However, I want more for you. My highest hope is that you will learn to use your difficult situation to transform in such a way that you will elicit the beauty in yourself through releasing energetic blocks on your body. At the end of this book, I aim to give you the skills to discover and navigate your spirit via your body, which is inextricably connected to Source Energy. In other words, this book is just the beginning of the benefits you will gain from this work. You are an infinite being, so there are infinite possibilities within you. This book attempts to point you in a fruitful direction toward those possibilities.

Each chapter will be accompanied by a mind-body

exploration, which could also be thought of as a meditation, that has been honed from learning and teaching my consciousness approach to life as a biofeedback specialist and subtle energy "healer" for over three decades. You see, I was born with this odd orientation. I seem to be highly aware of where my consciousness is parked and how it influences my experiences. Learning how to make my heightened awareness work *for* me, not *against* me, took me decades to figure out.

My first significant spiritual renovation occurred when I was twenty-one while obtaining a music degree. To my horror, as I was practicing my instruments, I realized I was performing worse instead of better after my long hours of practice. My fingers were not obeying my intentions. Soon, the ligaments of my joints started to pull apart, causing my joints to slide around in their sockets, putting pressure on my nerves and vascular system. I later learned that my joints were becoming hypermobile.

I was told by a prominent researcher in hypermobility that hypermobility can occur in less than 2% of the population, often afflicting women in their childbearing years. My body had declined consistently during the two years that it took for me to be diagnosed correctly. In the end, my condition was confirmed by a prominent researcher who told me, "*There is nothing medicine can do for you. Go home. Take anti-inflammatories, and you should tighten up by age 50.*" (At this writing, I am 56, and I am still hypermobile.) I remember I left his office crying and sat in my car on one of those egg crate cushions that older adults use because my hips hurt so bad. I was 23, but I felt 103. I had no idea how I was going to take care of myself. My desperation made me set an intention: *I would learn everything I needed to know to overcome my condition.*

Simultaneously, I did not know it then, but my physical challenges were exacerbated by a rude Kundalini awakening, causing all of my subtle energies to surge and flair. I had never heard the word "chi" before, yet it pulsed through my body, causing havoc. I would feel lines of energy that appeared to me like sparklers, traveling up and down energy lines on my body. This phenomenon was confusing for a young, introverted woman with a restrictive upbringing. I had no interest in spirituality, yet books and resources were being put in my path, encouraging me to ask more significant questions. Finally, when I read the book by a well-known Taoist and martial artist, BK Frantsiz, *Opening the Energy Gates of the Body*, I started to understand what was happening to me. I was in a subtle energy-purifying process. BK Frantsiz taught me there were ways to direct and stabilize my chi so I could run my energy, and my energy would not run me! Since then, I have never had a day where I did not consciously direct my chi. Generally, I don't even let 10 minutes pass at this point without directing my chi.

After about seven years, I was pain-free and trained myself to master my chi enough to run four miles a day. Eventually, I started wanting to share what I had learned, especially when I heard people talk about how their ailments inhibited their lives. In my mind, I would say to them, *"It doesn't have to be that way. There is another way!"* I wanted to tell them what I had been learning - but tell them what?!?! *"We have this invisible electricity inside our bodies, and if we learn how to direct it, we will have an entirely different life experience. Who would believe me? I may as well be talking about the Emporer's new clothes!"* I used to say to myself, *"Yeah, that and 50¢ will get me a cup of coffee*" (that is how long ago this was!) So, I spent many years not valuing the information I gleaned from inner space. Eventually, I dared to share by teaching my neighbor, and I have never looked back. It seems that the things I discover on the inside are beneficial not only to myself but to others. I have spent the last several decades learning to convey these profound truths. Ironically, they are under our noses, but we ignore them.

Usually, people only want to learn these skills after life has leveled them (like when confronting a problematic person.) When people are finally humbled enough, this work seems to be "the medicine" to heal them. After integrating this approach into your life, the information may be so revolutionary that you later look back at rendezvousing with this information as a "before and after" period of your life. However, that will only occur if you take this information to your cell tissue by performing the accompanying mind-body explorations. Eventually, you may even find yourself so hooked to this perspective that you want to continue studying by participating in a bank of **Consciousness Athlete** mind-body explorations that I have honed to expand my field and consciousness. After thirty years practicing this work, I can vouch that it just gets better. Love is infinite, so our only question is, *"Just how good do we want to feel?"*

Each chapter offers cognitive support for why we are approaching our energy fields as we are, but we can't stop at words for revolutionary transformation. Words are significantly removed from the experience. They are an incomplete teaching mechanism. As a well known spiritual text, *A Course In Miracles*, states, *"Words are just symbols of symbols."* This work seems to be a chapter in the eternal curriculum of earth-bound spirituality, so words can only be secondary to experience. As pretentious as that may sound, by the time you finish this book, you may agree with my presuppositions after you feel confirmation of this approach in your own energy field.

We will not address our "difficult person" until we have become calibrated to ourselves. We are sorely ill-equipped to face the uncertainties of a petty tyrant when we are not even familiar with our personal energetic patterns. Only after becoming intimately familiar with our spirit through our energy field will we discuss the gritty 3D world of interacting with frustrating petty tyrants.

This process can't be circumvented, so please refrain from skipping to the end of the book without doing the earlier prescribed mind-body explorations. Otherwise, you may as well just save money on this book and watch YouTube videos on similar topics. That would give you the same surface results, but I want more for you. I want you to know how to extract the valuable gifts your petty tyrant offers so you can try to enjoy your transformation, at least a little, in the process. I offer you tools to accelerate managing your initiation. Our goal is not merely to maneuver around your difficult person, but help you appreciate the grand journey you have already begun.

Although I have focused this book on addressing challenging relationships, you can use this mind-body explorations to face all your challenges. We are infinite conscious beings, and facing this world without embracing the more significant aspect of our nature causes us to leave money on the table when exploring solutions to tough problems. The energetic integrity skills you will learn can be applied to multiple situations, whether dealing with a challenging partner, relentless bills, or stubborn circumstances. You can transfer what you learn from this book to *all* your difficulties. It is the same process. As we discover how to use all our problems to recalibrate our energies toward wholeness, we learn how to enjoy all aspects of our lives more.

Petty tyrant friends offer us the unique irritation we need for purification. They are the proverbial grain of sand in our oyster that generates friction required to cultivate a pearl of great price and heightened consciousness. Jesus was one of the most prolific teachers of the pearl of heightened consciousness, as he referred to it as "*the kingdom of heaven.*" In Mathew 13:45-46, Jesus is recorded as saying, "*The kingdom of heaven is like a merchant looking for fine pearls. When he had found one pearl of great price, he went and sold all that he had and bought it.*" When you discover this Kingdom of Heaven within, you will understand why the merchant was willing to sell everything else for the value of this one pearl.

After years of mingling in the "pearl" of these sublime spaces, I understand why I saints and mystics have been reported to be so consumed in ecstatic union with the Divine that they needed to be force-fed and bathed for their protection.

This beauty is not just available to mystics, as it is closer to us than our breath; however, most of us have excessive mind chatter and too much density in our energy fields to allow it into our experience. When we learn how to access this beauty, it is a sublime refuge from all of the challenges we face, and it is available to all of us if we are willing to do the work to uncover it. (Tragically, it is also what everyone who suffers from substance abuse is seeking.)

I have often noticed in myself and others, there is a moment at the end of an initiation process where our energy has become so released and free, we feel exquisite expansiveness as our awareness surpasses our prior spread. This phenomenon is often accompanied by a flash of spontaneous gratitude. As I feel my field extending past where it has been, I often find myself taking a deep breath and savoring another delicate level of sweetness.

In this state, I usually have a spontaneous vision of ocean waves increasing their reach on the beach as a tide comes in, roaming up the coast and moistening sand it has not yet reached. As we expand into new spaces, we realize there is so much more to this journey than we have been told. Jesus also said, "*In my father's house are many mansions.*" (John 14:2). In this passage, he refers to different states of consciousness (mansions) where we all can dwell. In my first book, *Become a Consciousness Athlete - A Step By Step Program To Heighten Consciousness For Daily Happiness*, I illuminate this process and how we can soften the veil between this world and the next to live on earth, but with a touch of heaven. In this book, however, we will learn how to live in beautiful states not only despite our petty tyrants but because of them!

1
———

ANCHORING IN YOUR QUERENCIA

Take a moment now and bring
your petty tyrant to mind.
What happens in your body as you think
of your relationship?
Where do you clutch, grip, or grasp?
Do you feel a pulling-up sensation?

At every moment, sensations occur in our bodies, and we often don't question their meaning. Yet, in these subtle reactions lie the answers to some of our biggest questions in life. These nuanced cues are windows to our souls. We were often groomed to ignore them to make our responses socially acceptable. We learned to squelch the wisdom that was desperately trying to speak through our bodies' sensations. This response is incredibly unfortunate, as an entire universe is evolving within you, and if you are not attuned to your universe, you are missing out on the real story of you!

I am not being dramatic when I speak about inner space;

I have witnessed its mysteries for over thirty years. Years ago, I worked as a biofeedback specialist in a TMJ & Facial Pain Practice where I helped car accident victims release their muscular bracing that was exacerbating their TMJ pain. As I observed people connected to a traditional biofeedback instrument, galvanic skin response (GSR), which measures changes in perspiration, it would reveal a subtle yet powerful phenomenon we all experience. GSR instruments measure electrical changes in the skin caused by sweat gland activity in the fingers. It provides essential information about the body's physiological activation and excitement level in response to stimuli. I soon noticed that as patients moved their awareness down into their bodies, the pitch of the GSR would lower. I have always found it fascinating that our mind's locus of *internal* awareness in the body is so powerful it influences the *external* pitch of GSR.

To this day, every day, multiple times a day, I apply this knowledge to manage my consciousness. In thirty years, I have never tired of this process because I have understood that our locus of awareness, wherever it lands, dramatically influences our experience. When we come into command of our locus of awareness, we come into command of ourselves. When our awareness is undisciplined, we create havoc for ourselves. This book will teach you how to master your locus of awareness better. You will then be surprised at how many personal mysteries, including dealing with your difficult person, give up their secrets.

Interestingly, the pitch of the GSR increases when people experience a stressor, whether external or internal. So, for instance, if people are connected to a GSR, and there is a loud bang outside the door, the pitch of the GSR will increase, reflecting an increase in sweat in the body.

However, the same room can be completely tranquil, yet the pitch of the GSR will chaotically fluctuate, reflecting the patient's inner state. The pitch reveals a great truth that most people don't know: your body is eavesdropping on every-thing you think! You look like the picture of peace, yet all sorts of important things are happening in your body as you "do nothing" meditating.

I can recall one striking example of this phenomenon that occurred years ago. I was doing a GSR demonstration for a group of people. I asked the woman connected to the GSR to bring her locus of awareness to her abdomen. Instead of the pitch of the GSR lowering, it started to squeal sharply upwardly. I am highly skilled at directing awareness, so I gave her my usual queues honed after years of study to recover. Instead of the pitch lowering, it continued escalat-ing. She looked at peace with her eyes closed and hands facing upward in her lap. She certainly did not convey that something was alarming in her environment.

I stopped the demonstration and asked her what was happening inside of her. She said, *"Well, you asked me to move my awareness into my abdomen. My doctor told me that I have a growth in my abdomen the size of a grapefruit, so I am scheduled for an MRI this week. I am afraid if I move my awareness into my abdomen, I will make it real."* I explained to her that the stress hormones she was invoking while hesi-tating to settle down in her body would at least delay her from healing because the body, generally speaking, can't be stressed and healed simultaneously. This woman is a lesson to all of us. She demonstrated how we can look outwardly calm, yet inside, chaotic activity occurs that strongly influences our health and life. You might want to remember this the next time you meet with others. People may look calm, yet their internal worlds are often activated and edgy.

We mustn't ignore our inner life because it includes a ton of information critical for managing your relationship with your difficult person, and this book will help you access it. Your body offers wisdom that is entirely oriented around supporting you and no one else. It has no ulterior agenda. It is not trying to get you to buy something or vote for anyone that would not be in your best interest. It is your most crucial advocate because its only goal is to preserve you. Most people have never been taught to access their bodies wisdom, so they struggle much more than necessary. This work teaches you how to access your body's wisdom to choose more resourceful responses to your petty tyrant.

To access your body's wisdom, your locus of awareness has to be in your body first. That makes sense, right? This sounds like a simple approach, and it is simple. But I have to advise you, it is not easy! Unfortunately, many of us spend most of our time in what physiologists call "Sympathetic Dominance, " also known as the Fight or Flight response. This response is immediately triggered when we feel physical or emotional danger, which causes our bodies to mobilize physical resources to fight or flee from a predator. If we don't manage our bodies well, this response causes havoc in our relationships. For instance, if you are physically safe but having a difficult conversation with your spouse, the chemical hormones of the fight or flight response may activate, distorting your ability to interpret the conversation in a resourceful manner. The fight or flight response can distort our psychological disposition, causing us to overreact in relationships. Our relationships will be more stable if we learn to have difficult conversations without submitting to the fight or flight response.

Biofeedback training teaches us to maintain our locus of awareness in the body to remain calm while facing stressors. Over the years, I have witnessed only two people whose awareness I could not get reigned back into their bodies during their initial direct biofeedback instruction, but they were very instructive! One person was a woman who managed a Buddhist monastery and struggled with an eating disorder. The more I asked her to come down into her body, the more the GSR squealed until it left the audible spectrum. That means she was so agitated that the GSR went silent! I found this curious since she spent several hours a week meditating. How could someone leading a Buddhist monastery not know how to find her way back into her body when she was stressed?

After offering my usual instructions for these situations, I gave her space and left the room to help her orient herself to the GSR without my presence, thinking it would help her self-soothe without the pressure of a witness. This "performance anxiety" is common in my work, as about 60% of people want to be a "good student" for the trainer. When I returned to the room, she looked peaceful on the massage table, yet the GSR was still squealing wildly. I asked her, *"What are you doing?"* She said, *"I am doing my psychic protection process."* I told her, *"Well, your psychic protection process is stressing you out."* Her locus of awareness was stuck out of her body, and she resisted returning her awareness to it. She preferred to stay in her mind rather than feel her body.

It is also important to note that this person was struggling with an eating disorder, which often includes nuances of control issues that lead people to be unwilling to feel their bodies. One of the positive side effects of biofeedback is that it takes the destructive edge out of control issues. This work gives our will a highly constructive focus instead of using it to make our external environment or family members bend to our will. In this book, we will explore how you can manage your locus of awareness so you clearly understand what issues are yours to address and what are the issues of your difficult person to handle. I often say that most relationship problems are mismanaged nervous systems, so I will teach you how to regulate yours in this book. This work would work wildly better if, for some lucky reason, your difficult person would do this work with you. If you both do the mind-body explorations of this book, you can bypass destructive control issues and approach the heart of the issues much sooner.

Here is another fun, instructive fact relevant to our work together. Your body will tell me through the GSR which of your kids stress you out the most. I asked one woman to say her children's names. She listed, *"Jennifer, Riley, and Tom."* When she said the name Tom, the pitch of the GSR escalated. I said, *"So tell me about Tom?"* She responded, *"Tom is the problem child!"* She elaborated, telling me stories of how difficult it was to parent Tom. I told her, *"Notice how I knew to ask about Tom because the pitch of the GSR increased significantly when you mentioned him. Even though Tom is not in the room, he is influencing your nervous system now as if he is."* Understand that the same situation is happening with your difficult person. Each time you think of that person and feel stress, your body is activating as though he or she is in the room. After performing the mind-body explorations accompanying this book, you will learn how to halt the fight or flight response by altering your nervous system and energy field to attend to your relationship more skillfully.

I objectively refer to biofeedback instrumentation to support everything I have said. However, this book is for spiritual people, which gives me the privilege of addressing what is happening in our complicated relationships from a spiritually energetic perspective. It is challenging to refer to the spirit realm objectively, but I hope that through the mind-body explorations, you will discover that you can objectively work in your spirit. You will come to learn about your subtle energy landscape and where you are hemorrhaging your spirit to your relationships.

I refer to speaking to our spirituality as a privilege because Western culture discourages and often scorns spiritual conversations, now more than ever! Usually, as I led lectures and workshops over the years, I had to silence greater spiritual wisdom to stay in a secular lane. As I have witnessed the atheistic movement growing, which values rational intellect as supreme over spiritual pursuits, I see more and more people cutting themselves off from spiritual insight.

Being encouraged to eclipse ourselves from Spirit is just short of tragic to me, mainly because it is not surprisingly being accompanied by a steep increase in crippling anxiety, suicide, and substance abuse in our culture. In my opinion, the societal trend of separating ourselves from a larger benign intelligence significantly contributes to the alarming rise of suicides and drug overdoses. Many of us wither when we try to live while only attending to our physical nature. Without orienting around a spirituality, it is common to reach midlife and realize something is sorely missing. If people are unwilling to do the emotional work of filling the hole, they will most often fill it with drugs, gaming, media, alcohol, or food. In recent years, the number of senior citizens seeking addiction treatment in the United States has skyrocketed, along with suicidal attempts.

If we don't understand the more extensive nature of our journey here in this world, we tend to squander our precious lives, dissipating our life force through substances and watching incessant media. It is my highest hope that this book will encourage people to pursue an earnest spiritual path at any age. I suggest you don't take my word for any of my spiritual suggestions, but be sure to perform the mind-body explorations several times each to determine if this approach holds merit in your life.

As we start our first formal in depth discussion, I think it is important for us to consider the origin of our human spiritual condition. Our lives began when our eternal spirits took on the drag of a helpless physical infant. Our little bodies drastically limited access to infinite reality through our five narrowly restricted senses.

At this point in my studies, I understand that our goal for being here on earth is to play a "Divine Wake-up" game, which begins by forgetting that we are eternal as we acclimate to living in the physical plane. We don't forget our spiritual heritage entirely for our first seven years of life because we still feel connected to the spiritual world through our alpha and theta brainwaves. Alpha and Theta brainwaves help us to bridge our internal subconscious world to our external world, so they have a dreamier quality compared to our adult beta brainwave-dominated consciousness. As young children in an alpha-theta-dominated brainwave state, the idea that Santa Claus can be on a sleigh and travel around the world in one night makes perfect sense! Then, one day, as our brainwaves trend toward beta dominance, we begin developing concrete thinking, and suddenly, Santa Claus riding on a sleigh around the globe in one night sounds preposterous! As Santa Claus becomes a childish fantasy left behind, God is often left there, too. As we mature, our beta brainwaves dominate which makes us feel further away from our spiritual home. Spiritual practices help us return to brainwaves that are less loaded with adult analysis and responsibility and more anchored in the heart. If our spiritual path serves us well, we are grounded in the physical while simultaneously surrendering our small identity and remembering our infinite spiritual nature.

Many of us will not pursue spirituality willingly because we are so attached to earthly pleasures and pursuits. Hence, trials and tribulations show us the limitations of physicality, so many of us intuitively reach for something larger than our small selves, spirituality, to help us cope. Through this process, we feel more healed and whole as we slowly start to "remember" our spiritual heritage. Ideally, we begin recalling our larger mission. This effort to recognize our spiritual nature gives us more tools to play the "Divine Wake Up" game well.

Trying to solve problems without utilizing our eternal consciousness is like playing poker with one hand tied behind our backs. We are not playing with a full hand, so we suffer greatly! Identifying with our spiritual nature enables us to access an entirely new realm of information. The internationally known channel, Bashar, puts it this amusing way: *"When we try to solve a problem without utilizing our infinite consciousness, we act as "half-wits."* Truth! You are an eternal conscious being, and relying purely on physical reality means leaving money on the table in your life. Scientists tell us that our five senses filter out roughly 99.00001% of the information circulating around us. Think about that! We know closer to zero percent of what is happening around us than even 1% and yet we think we are so smart! *A Course In Miracles* immediately sets us straight toward a humble path on the first day of its 365-day spiritual curriculum, with themes like "*Nothing I see means anything*" and "*I don't understand anything I see.*" We must humble ourselves by acknowledging that our restricted five senses significantly filter our experience, which severely limits our ability to access to healing information embedded in the greater reality surrounding us. Spiritual truths can not be revealed when we are so confident of how to interpret the .00001% of the filtered reality around us.

A repetitive theme of this book will be that humility is your best friend to unlock your eternal wisdom. Jesus referred to the power of humility when he said the "*meek shall inherit the earth.*" He often invited people to experience humility so they could experience the "*kingdom of heaven within.*" This "kingdom" is within all of us, and as he often commented, it is "*in this world but not of it.*" He would often refer to children's humility as a model doorway to the kingdom of heightened consciousness. He suggested that this "pearl of great price (the kingdom of heaven within)" could be accessed by adults if we mimicked the unpretentiousness of children: "*Truly, I tell you, unless you change and become like little children, you will never enter the kingdom of heaven.*"

After studying consciousness for over thirty years, I can unequivocally say that we cannot access heightened states unless we let go of what we think we know. Humility is required because, in a humble state, you are teachable. You are not full of ego-personality, so you are open to resources your personality ego ignores to maintain control. We will return to this theme repeatedly throughout the book, as reducing self-importance is one of the primary tools for successfully engaging with a petty tyrant.

My goal is to help you find this humble pie delicious and learn to savor its flavor. Outlandish right? Not really. It is just the natural path of any advanced spiritual adherent who has reached the point where they know they are happier when they eliminate their ego selves to reap the benefits of being better calibrated with the Divine and their Higher Selves. The good news is that there is a way to work on cultivating humility without the embarrassment of getting an "egg on your face." In fact, after performing the mind-body explorations in this book, you may find accessing your humility quite enjoyable, and it is definitely the "safer" place to live from within ourselves. We will accomplish this by learning to stay in command of our spirit and anchoring our awareness in our bodies. We will de-emphasize thinking and embrace being. I intend to help you discern the difference and relish humility in a fun way. Each day, I practice becoming less so I can become more! You will understand the paradox more as we continue working together.

We have been discussing staying in command of our locus of awareness and establishing its home base in our bodies. I also mentioned that this is a simple but not easy process. According to the shamanic healing tradition, we can "lose" a portion of our soul (locus of awareness) when we undergo traumatic experiences. Our soul part will often return on its own. However, problems occur when individuals can no longer call their souls back home to their physical bodies. That is when shaman healers intervene. To retrieve the soul part, shamans move their awareness into a deep, loving space that holds no judgment for the patient. The shaman then "journeys back in time" to retrieve the patient's soul part and reunites it with the patient's spirit. The skills you acquire in this book will help you become your own shamanic healer to perform your personal soul retrieval. Through the mind-body explorations, you will skillfully call your spiritual power back to your body.

Sometimes, we may experience a soul breach and not even know it. As we continue living without a portion of our essence, we may find ourselves in monotonous daily struggles or complex relationships. We may repeat unhealthy patterns, get lost in addictions, experience frequent depression, feel haunted by fears of unworthiness, or struggle with insomnia and vague health conditions. You may not remember when your soul loss started, or you may know precisely when it happened because you remember something fundamentally shifting within yourself after the event.

Here is a game-changing concept of this book: It is possible that your petty tyrant has appeared in your life to help return a soul fragment that you do not realize is gone. If you are anything like me, you may resist this assumption when you first hear it. If you do, I understand entirely. As you will learn by the end of this book, I do not bend to spiritual law easily, either! I fight it like the rest of us! However, our discipline will be to explore the nonlinear wisdom of consciousness, not the rational 3-D mind. If you ever want to experience the spiritual state of oneness state, you would need to reconcile that your petty tyrant is actually your teacher.

You can get a glimpse of this perspective from people who experience near-death experiences. They commonly return to this world with a new appreciation for the people who have given them trouble. *A Course In Miracles* states this spiritual truth succinctly, *"It takes great learning to understand that all things, events, encounters, and circumstances are helpful. It is only to the extent to which they are helpful that any degree of reality should be accorded them in this world of illusion. The word "value" can apply to nothing else."* Tough words to grok, right? I get it! This book will help us easily grow into these truths and find a way to live harmoniously with them.

The work of this book and its accompanying mind-body explorations are versions of soul retrievals to help restore your spirit to its original fullness. As we practice these skills, we become happier because our spirit is critical to fueling well-being. If our spirit is trapped in old stories, we live in a "depressed economy mode." We simply don't have the excess energy required to confront familiar struggles or take on the challenge of establishing new habits.

When we anchor our mind's awareness in the body, our mind chatter, which is entirely responsible for our suffering, becomes silent. We become free to experience the purity of the moment without a story overlay. With our minds muted, we gain greater access to our spirit. New doors open within ourselves, resulting in flourishing health and creativity. My team and I observe these transformations repeatedly when people participate in **Resonant Peaceful City Projects**, sponsored by the non-profit I founded, NUMINOUS. As participants skillfully move their nervous systems into feeling greater love and wholeness, they gain new inspiring perspectives. We often witness how these insights offer people the strength and inspiration required to start new creative projects they have been delaying.

Wholeness is not whimsical, ephemeral, or vague. It is a

state of well-being that has undeniably palpable benefits. With training, it becomes a reliable, familiar place within ourselves, and we learn to settle for nothing less. We learn to tune to our wholesomeness, similar to how we would tune a guitar to play a beautiful song. We become highly skilled at recognizing when we are in a healthy state and when we are not.

When we acknowledge that we are not present, we have the skills to move our mind's awareness into the body, relax the constricted area, let go, and sink back into wholeness. As we let go physically, we let go emotionally. At first, our emotional patterns may be so well-entrenched that we find it extremely difficult to stop clutching the body when we think of our stressors. However, with training, we become skilled at remaining calm in our bodies as we review challenges. We understand that maintaining the integrity of our spirit is far more enjoyable than squandering our spirits through roller coaster rumination.

There is currently an explosion of research studying rumination, the process of continuously thinking about the same thoughts, which tend to be sad or dark. The habit of rumination can be dangerous. In her book, *Women Who Think Too Much*, Susan Nolen-Hoeksema discusses how people, especially women, often ruminate over the losses in their lives. They go round and round in their minds, over-thinking, and repeatedly ask themselves why people acted as they did. They often waste decades trying to make sense of things that will never make sense. To silence these endless ruinations, they usually try to mood alter through alcoholism, eating disorders, or other substance abuse. I have personally witnessed family members terrorize themselves with these mental patterns, literally until their death. The tyranny of the mind can be so severe I find it heartbreaking. I have come to understand why so many people resort to substance abuse to eliminate their suffering. Most people don't have enough of their spirit present enough to provide the grit required to stop ruminating.

If you master the mind-body exploration of this chapter, you can set yourself free from rumination forever if you are willing to undergo such training. As we hone the internal discipline to keep our awareness in our body, we develop the mastery to stop rumination in its tracks. I doubt it will be easy for you because we have become a culture that is frightened to feel our bodies, which is why we experience profuse suffering through anxiety disorders, substance abuse, obesity issues, insomnia, and chronic, unexplained pain. Feeling emotions and sensations is intimidating for a culture that lives in their heads and beyond. The mind-body explorations in this book train you in a mental-physical discipline that enables you to access resourceful states on demand.

The first place in the body where we will anchor our mind's awareness is in our lower abdomen, which martial artists consider the seat of power within us. As we cultivate this area with awareness, we gain impressive equanimity and strength. For centuries, eastern warriors developed an understanding of their power center to maintain emotional balance and sustained focus during war. When martial artists perform amazing feats, such as breaking boards with their feet or making their bodies so heavy that their opponents can't budge them, they accomplish these impressive stunts by staying in command of their awareness while hyper-focusing in their power center. In China, this center is called the tan tien; in Japan, it is called the Hara. The tan tien is in your lower abdomen, about 1.5 inches below your belly button. This area is also the center of gravity of the body.

We access more than just a physical center of gravity when we anchor our minds in the lower abdomen. We are also accessing the electrical power center of the body's acupuncture meridians. Acupuncture is an ancient Chinese medicine that has been proven to help various health conditions by triggering specific points on the body with needles. These points are on meridian lines, invisible energetic electrical pathways or channels that run through the body. For centuries, medical philosophies have espoused that "qi" (chi), or a vital life force, runs through these meridians, and anything that disrupts the smooth flow of qi is said to cause illness. Meridians are often stimulated to increase life force distribution with needles. However, it is important to know that we can also stimulate these meridians with our minds. The mind-body explorations of this book will teach you this discipline.

When we anchor our minds in the lower abdomen, we connect to our vital life force, which causes a healthy mental fertile stillness. The ancient Taoists referred to this area as the gate of life. They considered it the most crucial gateway for physical health and strength because all major acupuncture meridians travel through this point in the body. Mantak Chia, one of the world's leading authorities on the body's subtle energies, refers to the tan tien as the "fundamental power storehouse of the body." It is a center of potential. When you learn to tap into your tan tien with your mind, you feel it is a dynamic activity center. Subjectively, when you finally hone the internal mental discipline to park your awareness there, it may feel comforting, like "home."

The tan tien is considered a battery, elixir, and pump in

Eastern medicine. It is called a battery because it holds a charge of chi or life force. This philosophy assumes that we are all born with individual "natal chi" or energy stored in our tan tien. The tan tien is considered an elixir because it mixes the three significant types of subtle energies that pass through our bodies: chi, jing, and shen. These three energies are referred to as the "three treasures" because they are said to be responsible for our quality of life. Our health requires a blend of these three energies, similar to how most of us do best ingesting a combination of protein, carbs, and fats. We often become cranky and imbalanced if we try eliminating one of those food groups. We feel imbalanced if we also have an unevenness of the three energetic treasures. The work in this book will help you access and balance your three energetic treasures. Finally, the tan tien is also considered a pump because it pumps this elixir of energetic treasures out to the rest of the body to nourish us.

When we focus our awareness in our tan tien, we are physically balanced in the body, which interestingly means that we are also emotionally balanced. The tan tien is often considered the "seat of intention" because when we locate our awareness there, our intention becomes clear and unfettered without entanglements. There has been much discussion about intention in our culture recently, but the mysteries of intention have long been explored in the East. Martial artists intend to remain aware of their tan tien as much as possible. This understanding is so culturally ingrained in the East that if a Japanese child throws a temper tantrum, his mother may scold him by saying, "Hara. Hara!" meaning "Belly! Belly!" The Japanese mother would encourage her child to focus and become present and calm by anchoring his awareness in his abdomen.

Psychologist Karlfried Graf Durkheim spent the years between 1938 and 1947 studying Japanese culture before the West influenced it as it is now. He observed the reliance on the hara in everyday life. In his book *Hara, the Vital Centre of Man*, Durkheim describes the "matured inwardness" of individuals who spent years harnessing their mind's awareness to their hara. Life does not rattle these individuals. When anchored in the tan tien, they remain as calm as deep ocean waters, even if they can hear the noise of violent waves above them.

Durkheim also writes that people with a robust hara presence have a powerful influence over others. Often, people with solid hara are very sexy! They are charismatic and magnanimous, which draws people to them. Martin Luther King is an example of someone anchored in his hara, as evidenced by his relentless commitment to making his dream a reality, even while facing relentless resistance. Gandhi had great hara as well. These leaders steadfastly committed to social change and influenced others through unwavering grounded intentions. I figured it out one time, Gandhi was so disciplined with his mind, he essentially took down the British government after twenty one years due to his unwavering focus during beatings, prison stays, and hunger strikes. This invincible dedication is a natural outgrowth of being firmly grounded in the hara.

It is essential to note that just because people have a healthy hara, it does not mean they have purified their intentions. It only means that they are more effective in achieving their purposes. People like cult leader David Koresh had a strong hara as well. Occasionally, I see someone swagger with the confidence that only comes from being deeply anchored in the hara. Because of their charisma and ability to influence others, it is important to recognize that their magnanimous hara state of being does not mean to automatically trust them. They are still enjoyable to watch!

I teach people how to tether their minds' awareness in their hara by having them stand on two rubber discs found in most public gyms. When they establish their balance on these discs, they can become aware of the tan tien in their lower abdomen. Through this exercise, the tan tien becomes a tangible place in the body, not just a theoretical construct. After they become balanced on the discs by anchoring their awareness to their tan tien, I strategically ask them to tell me about their most stressful issues. As they start to share their internal struggles, they become imbalanced and wobble, often falling off the discs with laughter. Clients struggle to get back on the discs and remain upright while we pursue the topic further. It is a clear demonstration that when they are physically balanced, they are emotionally balanced.

Conversely, when they are emotionally balanced, they are physically balanced. As they cultivate a mental state of resourceful detachment while reviewing their challenge, their body starts to stabilize on the discs. Through contrast, they are shocked to become aware of the tangible physical results of losing their physical balance while mentally confronting a particular situation. You could also say that they "lose their power" as they become physically weakened while reviewing their stressors and thinking about petty tyrants.

In the first mind-body exploration of this book, we will learn how to maintain our awareness in our power center while thinking about challenging topics. As clients know how to remain in their tan tien while reviewing stressful issues, the quality of their thinking significantly changes.

Listening to what clients say changes about stressful topics while becoming more anchored in the tan tien is always fascinating. Their established perspectives change in real time. Their thoughts immediately pivot from victimized thinking to creative thinking. People become detached from their struggles. Their perspectives change to become more philosophical and transcendent. This integrated and innovative thinking is the signature they are thinking from localizing their more transcendent self poised in their tan tien (more on this later in the book.)

An example of individuals not anchored in their tan tien would be those who struggle with substance abuse. Because the addiction struggle often causes people to disassociate from their bodies, people with addictions do not have a firm awareness of their tan tien. Their minds are easily plucked by external stimuli, including trigger foods or addictive substances, so it is difficult for them to gather their awareness back in their body to gain control. In fact, clients who exhibit substance abuse often fall off the bubble discs when they talk about their addictive substance of choice. I even had to catch a woman as she fell backward off the discs after thinking about her passion for chocolate chip cookies! This loss of physical stability demonstrates to them that they lose their balance, both physically and mentally, in the presence of their substance or stressor of choice. They have a raw experience of how they surrender their power to the stressor, unable to maintain their center in its presence. I have witnessed the same phenomenon with the Galvanic Skin Response (GSR) biofeedback instrument. The GSR pitch often starts to squeal if people review their trigger substances while connected to the instrument.

The first goal of our work together will be to develop the

internal mental control to maintain a general awareness of our tan tien, especially in the presence of your petty tyrant. We think of cultivating this awareness as being rooted or tethered to our tan tien, the center of gravity of our bodies, which is also our connection to the earth. By remaining anchored in our lower abdomen, we have the strength of will to maintain composure, even when severely challenged. As we learn to tether our minds to the tan tien during stress, we find it enormously helpful to have a safe place to mentally land and so we feel emotionally stable. This inner stillness enables us to consider more appropriate and resourceful responses.

Consider how large trees remain stable through the storms of many seasons. The tree can only grow big and tall because it has a broad, rich root structure underneath. The roots of large trees ground them so well they do not bend or fall even in the harshest of winds. Similarly, we must gain roots in our tan tien to maintain our power. It is the center of gravity in the body, which similarly tethers us to the earth. In the mind-body exploration for this chapter, we will be working toward establishing a firm awareness of the tan tien, enabling us to remain resolute in the face of disruption as a tree stands tall during hazardous storms.

I am passionate about teaching these internal skills of remaining anchored in the body because I have witnessed how learning these skills change people's trajectories. I am saddened that this information remains so obscured because it causes people to struggle unnecessarily for decades, often complete lifetimes, so it brings me great pleasure to teach these skills, especially to children. I hope they will not need to spend years fighting against themselves, as I have witnessed many adults. I was blessed to have the opportunity to teach meditation in some of the most disadvantaged schools for many years. I love teaching children this esoteric skill of anchoring in their hara by having them face common real-life challenges.

One of my favorite lessons included bringing candy to school as an opportunity for students to tether their minds to their tan tien in the face of temptation. I purposely bought three bags—one for each type of sweet tooth—sweet, sour, and chocolate. If you have guessed that my approach to meditation is a little unorthodox, you are right! I don't linger on basic mindfulness practices too long before integrating more significant biofeedback and character-building themes by applying self-mastery skills to gritty real-life challenges. I do this because we learn the most when grappling with our most intimidating struggles. We may think we have control of our minds, but challenges reveal our mind's true weaknesses. The mind-body connection reveals our raw responses to challenges and astonishingly demonstrates that the body does not lie.

I pass out three small pieces of candy per child, with the instruction that if they can hold back from the temptation to eat the candies, I will give them three more small pieces 15 minutes later. In the interim, we discuss what is happening in their bodies as they are tempted to eat the candy. I remember one fourth-grader lamenting, in a comical voice, that she was "suffering" as she resisted the urge not to eat the candy in front of her. Her antics were funny at first. However, she continued long after the humor had worn off. I reminded her that the student beside her was not suffering because he was looking away from the candy, and neither was the child on the other side, who had hidden the candy under a piece of paper to avoid temptation. She was "suffering" because she had allowed her mind to anchor in her attachment to the candy. Next, as students struggle with temptation, I ask them to anchor their minds in their tan tien. I loved watching them transform before my eyes as I encouraged them to allow their rapidly growing self-respect to rise well into their awareness. Their backs straightened as they felt the pride of discovering their mental will power. I treasured those moments!

In the mind-body audio exploration I created to accompany this chapter, I will teach you how to hold a stance toward life grounded in your tan tien. Reviewing complex relationships, situations, and addictions, you will learn how to maintain your awareness steady in your tan tien and observe powerful shifts in your consciousness. While practicing this place of being, you may become "awed" by discovering what it truly means to be "empowered."

While cultivating this mastery, you may often feel a profound wave of self-respect and satisfaction move into your consciousness. Savor that feeling. Please get to know that place of anchored dignity within you. We need first to acknowledge these profound spaces within us to experience them more. They are our soul's lighthouse calling us home. Even if you have never experienced that state of consciousness before, you will immediately realize that it feels familiar because you can feel it is the "authentic you."

This powerfully poised place within us can be best described by a word in the Spanish language: Querencia. This word comes from the Spanish verb "querer, " meaning "to desire." It has also been described as a "homing instinct, a favorite place." The word is also used to describe a place in the bullfighting ring where the bull returns to gather his strength around him as the Matador threatens him. It is a space that is more psychological than physical in its boundaries. In his Querencia, the bull does not deflate in the presence of the Matador's sword. Instead, he puffs up and gathers his strength around him. In fact, if the Matador cannot entice the bull out of its Querencia, it means the Matador must go to the bull and enter into the area of greatest danger to the bullfighter. For once in its Querencia, the bull now controls the situation. This is an excellent metaphor for us to model when facing problematic people; we are often best served by pausing to gather our strength and find our Querencia within us before interacting with them.

Establishing our querencia in the tan tien is the first skill we will develop to significantly change our interactions with our difficult person. We will review different challenging situations to gain greater mastery of our spirit by anchoring our awareness of the Querencia of our tan tien. Another way to describe this process is that we will become "Spiritual Warriors" as we learn to manage ourselves. Often, spiritual people shun the concept of Spiritual Warriorship because of an assumed conflict it conveys. However, that is because they need help understanding its true meaning. The term spiritual warrior is used in Tibetan Buddhism for one who combats the universal enemy: self-ignorance. According to Buddhist philosophy, the ultimate source of our suffering is a lack of self-knowledge. Through deep fundamental self-awareness, we learn to reduce our ignorance and thus reduce our suffering. As we learn to cultivate the courage to analyze ourselves objectively, warts and all, we become spiritual warriors. We learn to assess how well we are investing our spirit and how we are using challenges as an opportunity to stay in command of our power, not to squander it.

When we firmly establish internal power, our commerce with our world shifts. This process is the central theme of this entire book. We will use our petty tyrant challenge to eliminate self-ignorance and reduce suffering for ourselves and our petty tyrant, changing the whole relationship frame. During this process, we see our petty tyrants as teachers who mirror how we can better manage our spirit. Carlos Castaneda nicely wrote about this powerful shift in perspective: *"The basic difference between an ordinary man and a warrior is that a warrior takes everything as a challenge, while an ordinary man takes everything as a blessing or a curse."* In this book, we will take the challenge as an opportunity to rid ourselves of self-ignorance to reduce our suffering. We begin gaining greater mastery and control by anchoring in the Querencia of our tan tien, as we intentionally create a calmer internal environment that fosters personal power. This philosophical and physical shift enables us to consider a broader range of responsive behaviors while it strengthens feelings of embodied empowerment.

Before we anchor in the tan tien, we will begin by aligning with our body's vertical power current of energy by sitting as upright as possible. To become aware of our tan tien, we want to feel balanced in the body from front to back and from left to right. We will also begin by aligning with an imaginary plumb line, starting about 1.5 feet above our head, descending down through our bodies, between our legs, and ending below our feet, with an imaginary weight at the end anchored in the center of the earth. We will practice holding our heads high and shoulders back with great dignity. As the founder of Shambala Meditation, Chogyam Trungpa Rinpoche taught us; we attempt to sit in meditation with *"good head and shoulders."*

I have also helped young students in school find the regal space of their plumb line. I invite them to sit with their legs crisscrossed on the floor. With their permission, I run my thumb up their spine between their shoulder blades. Their shoulders splay back and down, and more than once, the room of students quietly gasps at the majestic beauty and dignity that naturally springs forth from the model student. We are all touched by this experience.

When fully present, we naturally hold our heads and shoulders with this majestic air. The research of psychology professor Richard Petty reveals that when we hold our heads up, we have an easier time thinking "empowering, positive" thoughts about ourselves. Conversely, when our heads are down, we are more likely to experience "hopeless, helpless, powerless, and negative" feelings about ourselves. Petty surmises that the marked increase in time spent sitting in front of computers and looking down at smartphones may be a significant contributing factor to the rise of depression in recent years. Because vision is lowered and eyes gaze down so much, it is easy to become self-centered. Our mood may also be negatively altered when we slump because when our head droops, our chest collapses, severely restricting our breathing. This lack of oxygenation in the body can lead to lethargy and depression. To combat these disempowering feelings, I invite students to walk confidently, with their heads up, and eyes forward, as if they know where they are going. When we lift our heads and see others, we take attention off ourselves. We naturally create an open heart, which is the subject of our next chapter.

Enjoy finding new spaces within yourself during the first mind-body exploration, *Anchoring in Your Querencia Through Challenge,* because it will connect you to your inherent dignity and worth. I recommend that you sit in a chair for the first few times you perform each meditation. Also try to transfer your learning. Continue exploring this new orientation in real life situations, for instance, as you walk into work, have difficult conversations with your spouse, or coax your resistant teenager. Explore these fertile states of being and how they offer you a more extensive and empowering range of responses. Feel appreciation for yourself as you find the courage to explore these spaces, and be sure to show tremendous respect for your choices (more on that in later chapters). When people try to rattle you, make it a game to see how much you can remain anchored to your abdomen as you breathe deep down into your tan tien, filling it like a bellows. In the face of a tempting food or drink, practice keeping your awareness rooted in your tan tien and do not allow your consciousness to hemorrhage toward the temptation.

Please be very clear: until you master this discipline, it will be difficult. It could take years. Remember, I have said, "This work is simple but not easy." Frankly, learning this skill under stress is like learning how to pull a parachute while jumping out of a plane! Your energy may have never been routed this way, or at least not for many decades. When I demonstrate this with the GSR or the discs, people often comment, "*This is a lot of work!*" as they labor to maintain the discipline. I usually recognize when people struggle and say to them, "*You are hanging on for dear life right now, aren't you?*" They often exhale, release their shoulders, and say with relief, "*Yes! This is hard!*" So, go easy on yourself.

It will not be easy, but your effort is worth it. Every time you attempt to maintain awareness of your tan tien, whether you feel you have been successful or not, you will have gained an enormous step toward mastery. This is similar to the way lifting weights builds strength. Each time you raise a weight, you become stronger. Each time you harness your locus of awareness to your tan tien, your mind strengthens.

To acknowledge how powerful your mind is, always notice how you feel before you begin a mind-body exploration. Then, compare these feelings to how you feel at the end. People often acclimate to these enhanced states so quickly that they forget where they began. Then they say things like, *"It didn't work"* or *"It didn't last."* If you feel remarkably different between the beginning and end of the mind-body exploration, than this work worked! Altering your locus of awareness made a profound shift within your body that would not have happened if you were unwilling to discipline your mind through this mind-body exploration. Results "lasting" is squarely up to you. How committed are you to disciplining your mind to maintain the change?

Some people may not be up for this challenge, which is understandable. It will require grit and will. It requires that you take a stand for yourself and your happiness. It requires you to honor yourself and consider yourself worthy of relentlessly pursuing your well-being. As I often say, this type of grace is costly. You may need to read this book repeatedly and practice the internal skills hundreds of times to sustain your efforts. However, I guarantee that if you come into command of your awareness and stand internally to maintain your physical and emotional center, your self-respect will grow immensely. I urge you to honor yourself in this way. It is only the beginning of a more empowering orientation to life.

If you practice anchoring in your Querencia, I guarantee your confidence will bloom. You will master your mind more, and your innate self-respect will emerge into your consciousness. Your decision-making will improve without having to white-knuckle healthier choices. You will want to do the right thing because it feels like the right thing in the deepest part of your being, so you will no longer be willing to betray yourself. You will become addicted to feeling aligned and no longer be willing to give up this feeling of inherent honor for anything. Eventually, your environment will respond to your heightened integrity and alignment, and you will realize you had access to this space within you all along!

You can find the audio mind-body exploration,
Anchoring in Your Querencia Through Challenge at
NuminousOnline.org/pearl
Enter the password: pearl

2

HEALING HEARTS

Take a moment now and bring your awareness
to the center of your chest.
What happens in your heart as you think
of your petty tyrant?
Do you feel your chest muscles tighten,
creating a heart wall?
Do you find yourself telling stories
about this person?

Please have performed the mind-body exploration of chapter one at least five times before proceeding to this chapter. The words of this book are just pointers. They are not your highest wisdom. Your most valuable wisdom will come from within as you learn to become sovereign within yourself. Many have heard the adage, "All answers come from within." Yet, most of us have yet to be taught how to cultivate an internal environment that allows wisdom to emerge, so we endlessly roam outwardly for answers, often running in circles. This book is written to help you set up an internal environment that accelerates your ability to access your personalized wisdom. Your situation is complicated. There are no books about your relationship's unique nuances; The wisdom you need can only be accessed by diving into your soul. Each chapter of this book will take you deeper into your being to access your customized reservoir of wisdom.

After practicing the mind-body exploration, *Anchoring In Your Querencia Through Challenge*, I presume you found new spaces within your personal environment. I would bet that an insight or two emerged. Maybe you felt greater strength, dignity, and detachment. Perhaps you noticed you had access to new resources to help you relate to your petty tyrant. Creative problem-solving probably emerged as well. It is also possible that you learned how undisciplined your mind is because it was challenging to maintain your locus of awareness in your body, especially while imagining being in the presence of your petty tyrant.

I made these educated guesses after teaching literally thousands of people through biofeedback presentations on how to master inner space for almost thirty years. I have witnessed the potent alchemy of this work. I know that peace is the birthright of all of us, which is why I have often donated massive resources of my time, talent, and financial resources to share this type of work with as many people as possible through our Resonant Peaceful Cities Project sponsored by the nonprofit I founded, NUMINOUS. There is magic within us, yet until we learn how to access it, we continue to struggle massively as a species. I have dedicated my professional life to mitigating some of our unnecessary suffering.

As we proceed, continue to draw your locus of awareness

to your tan tien as much as possible because we will build on that skill now. Keep going. I have not met anyone who has mastered this work. Even committed martial artists who continually hone their locus of awareness can only keep it anchored in their tan tien 50% of the time, at best. So, please be patient with yourself.

A well-known phrase in Tibetan Buddhism, "The fruit as path," applies to my approach in this book. It refers to an understanding that merely feeling the results of a goal accelerates achieving it. If our goal is peace, we start with peace. If our goal is love, we begin with love. Another well-known proverb describes our process well, "*The wind never blows in favor of a ship with no destination.*" Using this approach, we need to know how we want to feel resolved with our petty tyrant so we can begin there. Otherwise, we may lose valuable time meandering in a sea of disorienting, troubling emotions.

Traditional thinking tells us to delay feeling happy until specific outer circumstances occur. However, if we wait until our outside world changes to feel positive feelings, we may never allow ourselves to feel cheerful. I don't know about you, but I never enjoyed unnecessary delayed gratification. Instead of waiting for external circumstances to change before we feel happy, we will begin with cultivating the internal spaces we want to inhabit in our challenging situation, such as love, honor, dignity, and integrity. We will start with the result of how we want to feel in the body and then face our external world with our internal feeling goal.

Through this process, you pull your Spirit back from unhealthy rumination so that it is present to choose more enlightened actions. Understand that each time you discipline your locus of awareness by directing it where you want it to be, it is similar to doing another repetition of weight lifting at the gym. Each time you lift a weight, your muscles get stronger. Each time you draw your locus of awareness under your control, your mind becomes more robust so that difficult circumstances don't sway you.

You may have noticed in the last mind-body exploration that as you aligned your body in such a way as to lift your chest and eyes while anchoring in the tan tien, you felt a surge of dignity. That dignity wave emerges as the body aligns correctly because your life force energy flows through your acupuncture meridians unimpeded. As your life force runs through its appropriate channels, your soul can return online with your internal awareness, and you immediately recognize your inherent worth. In later chapters, we will discuss more about how honoring our worth, paradoxically while eliminating our self-importance, is a vital, delicate process of this high teaching.

In the mind-body exploration for this chapter, we will now explore another vital location on your vertical power current: your heart center. Poets and theologians have written about the power of the human heart since the beginning of the written word. Often, the most popular movies depict intricate love stories. On Valentine's Day, candy-shaped "hearts" are shared among friends, families, and beloveds to symbolize love. Yet, still, it would behoove all of us if the masses better understood the fundamental energetic technology of the human heart.

In my earlier book, I explore how an unfettered heart enables us to move into greater heart coherence, which allows us to feel "happy for no good reason." In that book, I explore heart coherence and the research of the Institute of Heartmath; I discuss what I refer to as a *"Dynamic Lifestyle of forgiveness."* (Spoiler alert: if you want to "be happy," just release your heart!) However, in this book, we will take heart work to a whole new level. We will skillfully strive to "empty" our hearts so that a greater loving wisdom that benefits all emerges.

We will find anchoring in our hearts may be a little easier than anchoring in our tan tien, but not by much! LOL. Many people read the Heart Sutras or learn about the research of the Institute of Heartmath and reflexively set an intention, *"Ok, so this is simple. All I need to do is stay in my heart, and all will be well!"* Yet, almost immediately, they are confronted with real-life complex challenges illuminating the precariousness of their simple proposed orientation. Soon, they find themselves in double binds where their hearts and minds are warring. The spiritual adherent says, 'I just want to love and stay in my heart, and yet, this person's behavior is so egregious it makes it impossible for me to love him/her!"

If you find yourself saying something similar to yourself, know that you have now entered the realm of the petty tyrant spiritual curriculum. Spiritual Facebook memes have absolutely no application in this territory! If you are dealing with a severe petty tyrant (we will classify them later), you are "not in Kansas anymore." You are now being called to operate from the emptiness of transcendent love, which is far more advanced.

You may be asking, *"What is a petty tyrant?"* A petty tyrant is a term made famous by Carlos Castaneda in his book *The Fire From Within.* He referred to a petty tyrant as *"a tormenter, someone who either holds the power of life and death over warriors or simply annoys them to distraction."* Essentially, a petty tyrant is someone in your life who feels like, no matter how hard you try, you can't get your relationship to work. It's someone that you could read all the relationship books available and impeccably apply their wisdom, but the relationship does not improve for some reason. You could pray, sending peace and love, yet your relationship seems immune to well-meaning intentions.

Let's review the people in your life now to discern whether or not you have a classic petty tyrant and where they may fall on my homemade <u>Friend-to-Tyrant Scale</u>. Understand that if you are confronting a genuine petty tyrant, managing this relationship probably requires an entirely different skill set than you have been utilizing. You can't rely on your regular commerce with the world because the role of the petty tyrant in your life is for you to unearth the dormant power you have not been using. Don Juan, the master shaman in Casteneada's book, said, "*My benefactor used to say that a warrior who stumbles on a petty tyrant is a lucky one!*" You may not feel lucky now, but on the other side, you will learn how this relationship's precise blend of difficulties facilitates phenomenal growth, which a friendly person simply can not offer! As Don Juan quipped, "*self-importance can't be fought with niceties.*"

Later in the story, we learn how Don Juan even willingly returned to work with his petty tyrant to use it to demonstrate his level of emotional mastery to himself. Please be clear: Current experts do not recommend tempting fate with capricious petty tyrants; however, it was a highly instructive opportunity in the context of Don Juan's learning goals. One takeaway we can utilize from this approach is that you may want to start reframing your petty tyrant relationship in such a context by making emotional mastery a "game." How much can you stay in command of yourself during your most vulnerable challenges?

When we have learned basic biofeedback and subtle energy skills, we have many resources to accomplish this goal, and the mind-body explorations in this book are designed to help you gain these self-regulation fundamentals. For instance, years ago, a biofeedback mentor told me that he challenged himself to stay eerily calm as he sat in Universal Studios staring at a screen of 3D Special Movie effects that appeared to be coming straight at him! Seeing how you can remain calm can become a game of mastery. Similarly, I have found myself "heavily meditated" at times when I thought that I should possibly be more upset with the situation I was facing. Call us biofeedback geeks, but you may also find joy in becoming a Biofeedback Geek by the end of this book.

I will help you assess whether you have an absolute petty tyrant or are just experiencing the regular bumps and bruises of sharing life with others. Imagine a scale from one to ten, where the person at number one would be your best friend. You can tell this person your worst stuff, and he or she will still see the best in you.

A person around a number five on our scale would be someone with whom you occasionally encounter problems. You both don't always see things perfectly eye to eye, but you have found a way to agree and disagree. You find a way to get along even with your differences. This is the kind of person where if you read a book on improving relationships and applied the professional advice, it would actually work. Both of you are strong enough within yourselves to discover ways to bob and weave as you cohabitate together.

Petty tyrant territory starts at number eight on our

Friend-to-Tyrant scale. Let me give examples of what it is like to be involved with a petty tyrant. You may immediately notice that the relationship has an entirely different emotional tenor. It will often feel like walking on eggshells, so you are always second-guessing yourself. The petty tyrant constantly addresses peccadillos within you while blindly ignoring their own glaring flaws. They hold you accountable to high standards but apply a different merit system to themselves.

One definite sign of a petty tyrant relationship is that you pity them while they are hurting you or someone else. Feeling pity is a powerful indicator that you are in a relationship with this type of person. In the words of Dr. Martha Stout author of *The Sociopath Next Door*, "*The best clue is, of all things, the pity play. The most reliable sign, the most universal behavior of unscrupulous people, is not directed, as one might imagine, at our fearfulness. It is perversely an appeal to our sympathy.*" Dr Stout elaborates later in her book, "*When deciding whom to trust, bear in mind that all the combination of consistently bad or egregiously inadequate behavior with frequent plays for your pity is as close to a warning mark on a conscience-less person's forehead as you will ever be given.*" If you are feeling pity for someone hurting you, you could bet that that person is a toxic or a high-conflict person.

A petty tyrant is someone with whom you never really feel at ease. Often, if they are talking, you don't quite believe them. You usually walk away from exchanges with more questions than answers, constantly feeling like there is more to the story. Something about this person always leaves you on edge.Technically, the official definition of a petty tyrant is that they somehow hold power over you. It could be temporal power like a job, or a relationship power like a spouse. It could be any relationship you cannot quickly vacate or remove yourself from, so you feel trapped.

This book will specifically address those people in our lives who are between 8-10 on this <u>Friend-to-Tyrant Scale</u>. Review your life now and see if you have a relationship that meets this 8 - 10 criterion. Suppose you don't; enjoy the respite! However, I would not want you to think you wasted your investment in this book because the skills you learn from this book can be applied to any "impossible" situation that makes you feel trapped, such as finances or neighbors. I intend to help you see the unique value of this difficult person or circumstance so you can mine the situation for profound gifts possibly being offered to you. Because when we master the tyrant relationship, be it a person or a circumstance, you will eventually probably be thankful for the learning, albeit, I will admit, begrudgingly at first (I know, I have been there!). But with more distance from the resolved situation, you will be grateful that you retrieved your soul parts. You may even feel that it was an even trade in the end. You handled some grief, yes, but you feel more whole and integrated because of it.

One of my favorite ways to describe this change in dynamics was an old story nuanced in the Harry Potter books. In this story, a gentleman is given the cloak of invisibility. This cloak made him invisible to "Death," so he lived a long, robust life. When he finally decides it is time for him to die, he chooses to remove the cloak of invisibility, and Death soon greets him. The story's final sentence is this: *"They greeted each other as friends, and they left as equals."* Sit with this idea for a moment. Imagine sitting with your petty tyrant as both a friend and an equal.

After you apply the skills in this book, even after all the

hell they put you through, it is highly possible that you may become both friends and equals. This will only occur if you take the opportunity they offer you as an invitation to mastery. However, mastery requires eliminating all victimization, even while not allowing yourself to bury your head in the sand to avoid it. In the next chapter, we will discuss how we need to see the situation clearly for you us to resolve it that effectively. Accountability is rarely a popular option, so you will need to feel comfortable being on your own for a while as you move toward integrity. This is a significant part of the petty tyrant curriculum. Standing in your inner knowing, even though others may not agree, especially your petty tyrant.

Keep your head up and persevere. You may eventually see your relationship from an even broader, more breathtaking perspective as you experience them holding absolutely no power over you. You will see how, through the challenges, they pulled out the highest and best from you because you knew the curriculum and played it well. Through the friction, you became the proverbial polished pearl cultivated due to a grain of sand in an oyster. As an oyster becomes irritated from the annoying presence of sand, it throws a mantle over it, which is the mother of pearl. The oyster continues to throw mantles over the sand as it keeps layering it, resulting in a lovely, gorgeous pearl that society considers valuable. I will refer you back to this concept often as we proceed. Getting polished by irritant exposure is never fun, so keeping our goal in mind is best to persevere through the misery.

A quote from a well-known spiritual book, *A Course In Miracles*, helps me reframe the difficulties I face: "*It takes great learning to understand that all things, events, encounters, and circumstances are helpful. It is only to the extent to which they are helpful that any degree of reality should be accorded them in this world of illusion, in fact the word value can apply to nothing else."* You can begin now to significantly alter the situation by pulling back your power and asking yourself, *"How am I being asked to feel more whole? What am I learning that is valuable in this situation?" How do I integrate relying on a greater intelligence that connects us all rather than my small egoic perspective? How is this an opportunity for me to access dormant power within myself?"*

Later in this book, we will discuss how it is best to get out of petty tyrant relationships as soon as possible, with a forgiving heart. We will also discuss common scenarios where people are unable to leave (here are a couple excruciating examples: being the parent of a sociopath or suddenly working under a new tyrannical boss in a company where you have worked twenty-eight years, but you can't retire until thirty years). You would be surprised to learn how many of these situations occur. You may not have the option to run, so this book offers options for managing your complex situation. But, before you take an easy out, are you really trapped, or could you leave? If you find that you are in a toxic relationship, be sure to explore every option to leave first!

You won't believe me yet, but after facing at least a dozen petty tyrant people in my life (and I have had some 11's!) I understand why Don Juan's teacher used to say that a warrior who stumbles on a petty tyrant is a lucky one. He felt the growth was so valuable and life-enhancing that if you didn't have a petty tyrant, it was worth finding one! Because there is no better teacher than having to hold your power in the unknown of a capricious, unaccountable, petty tyrant. I can vouch for this understanding; I attribute my petty tyrant parade for offering me initiations on how to use my powerlessness as a doorway to mastering cavorting with the Divine. This highly beneficial relationship continues long after the tyrant is gone.

I knew I had hit a basic level of mastery of this work when I was wrongfully accused by an employee who refused to be accountable for his job description. It could have looked daunting for me as his supervisor. He was very clever in his deceptions. However, I remember leaving the meeting with management executives and this employee, and my boss said to me in admiration, "*Well, I don't have to worry about you!*" I had no idea what she was referring to, so I asked, "*What do you mean?*" She proudly stated, "*You held your own in there!*" I didn't think I had done anything remarkable, so I said, "*I did? What do you mean?*" she described how I had strategically taken down the employee's false accusations with adroit skill. I really did not put it all together until later, because it was just the outgrowth of years of practice. I had just followed a petty tyrant formula I had constructed. I took my ego out of it and remained humble and calm as I set up situations for him to reveal his lack of accountability which he walked through nicely (although I must admit, I was subtly shaking!).

One final point I would like to share that is critically important when dealing with petty tyrants. Petty tyrants are unwilling to be accountable, but you must be impeccable. That sounds horribly unfair, I know, but that is the petty tyrant script. They will reveal your weaknesses, so you must find your weaknesses first and eliminate them or they will exploit them. It is best to be 100% honest with yourself and Source Energy in this matter because, as we have discussed, they snuff out breaches of integrity and hold them against you, which only confuses and delays the desired resolution.

I will paraphrase a vignette that Carlos Castaneda writes in his book, *The Fire From Within*, about how his teacher, Don Juan, faced his violent tyrant under dangerous circumstances while he became impeccable unto himself. This is a story of extremes, but we sometimes grasp things easier when we observe stark contrasts. As you will learn in the next chapter, I do not suggest this approach with most petty tyrants; however, this is an instructive tale worth retelling.

Don Juan was a young, poor migrant worker (I believe in the southwest United States). He went to town one day and applied for a job with a supervisor of a large estate. The supervisor told Don Juan that his job would offer him food, shelter, and a generous salary for caring for a woman's estate. Feeling like he won the lottery, he excitedly accepted the position.

Don Juan followed his new supervisor to the home and quickly learned the frightening truth. He was trapped on a large estate on the outskirts of town with his new supervisor, who he now realizes is a thief and a killer. Don Juan learns that he is taking the place of many young men before him, who were violently treated and worked to their deaths. He also learns that his most recent predecessor died within the last twenty-four hours. Don Juan was hired to take his place until his own inevitable savage demise. Even the kitchen help knows Don Juan is on borrowed time. They encourage him to eat as much as he can, because they know the cruel supervisor will work him to death and find another naïve kid to take his place. Don Juan is petrified.

Don Juan works hard with anger in his belly. Eventually, he is beaten within an inch of his life. By a twist of fate, although he is almost fatally wounded, he gets off the estate and onto the road. A benefactor finds him and nurses him back to health. Eventually, his benefactor asks, "*What happened to you?*" Don Juan describes his experience with the cruel, sadistic sociopath who beat him and left him to die. As Don Juan tells the benefactor his tale of being viciously assaulted, the benefactor (also a shaman) responds, "*Wow, do you have any idea how lucky you are that you found the most amazing petty tyrant? Even a vicious jumbo one!*" Don Juan is shocked at his disregard for his almost murderous experience and asks, "*What do you mean I am lucky? I almost died!*" Don Juan explains the value of petty tyrants and how they can be utilized to eliminate our weaknesses and prepare us to face the unknown with freedom in our hearts. (author's note: I have completely paraphrased this dialogue above this text for brevity. Please see *The Fire From Within*, by Carlos Castaneda for the complete story).

The Shaman benefactor brings Don Juan back to life, teaching him to hold his dignity while facing challenges, including treacherous people. Don Juan is taller, stronger, and more filled out two years later. When Don Juan is healed and wise enough, his benefactor encourages Don Juan to return to the estate to face his former tormentor. Don Juan is ready to apply all he has learned to use the situation with the vicious, petty tyrant to test his skills of harnessing his power. (Again, we will discuss in the next chapter why this is not a good approach for most petty tyrants. I tell this story for instructional purposes only).

Don Juan returns to town and applies for the same job. Because he has matured, the tyrant does not recognize Don Juan. The supervisor returns him to the estate under the same pretense, and the cycle begins again. The supervisor plans on working on him to death while stealing Don Juan's salary from the lady of the house, who has no knowledge of this lethal cycle.

Only this time, Don Juan enters the home with his eyes wide open, remembering the terrifying experience. He knows how his story is supposed to end. Instead of confronting the situation as a young, naive boy, he confronts the situation as a highly skilled warrior. Through his shamanic training, he has adopted the empowered stance of a soldier. He now knows not to surrender his power. He knows that mastery of the situation means remaining in charge of his Spirit no matter the difficulties or beatings facing him.

So, what is this "empowered stance" he was trained to adopt? It was not to protect himself from physical threats using might and muscle. The Shaman taught him that the most powerful stance he could adopt would be eliminating "self-importance." Don Juan immediately recognizes the wisdom of eliminating his pride. He knows he has to sublimate any emotionality and adopt a humble disposition so he can furtively study his supervisor's behavior. Don Juan also knows he must study himself with the same keen awareness so he can immediately become aware of any excess emotionality that would cause him to put himself in even more danger.

Don Juan understands he has to be tightly disciplined to survive, even while he is being treated poorly (remember, I am only telling this story for instructive purposes. I do not recommend this approach!) His benefactor taught Don Juan to completely sublimate his self-importance so he can keep his mind sharp enough to see opportunities for escape as they presented themselves. His benefactor elaborated, "*self-*

importance is our greatest enemy because it weakens us. When we feel offended by the deeds and misdeeds of our fellow man, our self-importance requires that we spend most of our days offended by someone; however, without self-importance, we are "invulnerable."

It is important to note, Don Juan's teacher instructed him to lose his self-importance out of strategy, not weakness. As we apply this wisdom to our lives, it becomes obvious how often our unchecked emotionality gets us into trouble. We soon realize that we can move about more freely if we proceed through this world with a lower emotional profile. (The Stoics knew all this well!) We learn not to betray ourselves with excessive emotion when we feel trapped to avoid suffering the consequences of our undisciplined emotions. We intend to accept the learning opportunity offered to us and face the difficult situation with humility and dignity while not succumbing to resentment or victimization. Through this line of reasoning, it becomes evident to Don Juan that losing his self-importance is critical to his survival.

An iconic psychiatrist, Thomas Szasz, who challenged many norms of psychiatry, refers to the correlation between humility and learning when he wrote: *"Every act of conscious learning requires the willingness to suffer an injury to one's self-esteem. That is why young children, before they are aware of their own self-importance, learn so easily; and why older persons, especially if vain or important, cannot learn at all."* To rephrase Szasz's quote, we are so "full of ourselves" as adults that we can't accept new information nearly as fast as children, so it takes us considerably longer to learn (or even to "see the obvious.")

Don Juan's benefactor admits eliminating self-importance is tricky business because self-importance brings out both the best and worst in people. If we have our dignity, we know we are worthy of being treated with honor. However, the second self-importance inflates just a bit into entitlement or pride; it turns on us, and our petty tyrant will often quickly call it out! This paradox is a slippery slope. It is best addressed through the mind-body explorations because only in a deep state of humility generated by being anchored in your body can you determine the appropriate balance of healthy versus unhealthy self-importance. Healthy pride is good; however, when our egos get bruised, and we want to "put someone in their place" or teach them a lesson by "making them wrong," our egos will often be humiliated by our tyrant without boundaries.

Eliminating toxic self-importance reminds me of the title of a book by Tara Singh, *Keep the Bowl Empty*. The book encourages us to release ourselves from unnecessary mental patterns that apply pressure. We are encouraged not to be so enamored with our own version of stories. As we progress along the petty tyrant training, we learn to strategically empty ourselves of our stories to respond to our environment more appropriately. We know not to waste energy being swayed by negative feelings, so we see how to remove ourselves from the situation skillfully.

Here is a caveat. Don't overshoot it! Remember that you're releasing your self-importance because you do not want to squander your power; it's not because you are willing to be a humiliated victim or you "deserve" it. Do you understand the difference? You are not eliminating your self-importance because you're ready to accept your fate of becoming an unworthy doormat. The exact opposite. You choose this approach because you are no longer willing to squander your power on emotions that weaken you. We will be sure to revisit this topic when we discuss healthy self-importance in chapter four.

The way of the Shaman is to be impeccably precise with how to spend your energy. Shamans refuse to send their Spirits on escapades that will not strengthen them. It is understood that all of their life force should be used resourcefully and not wasted in activities and discussions that weaken them. Non-productive behaviors and self-talk consume enormous energy, and shamans strive to keep as much of their power for themselves. Their banked power is used to finance extraordinary lives. In the mind-body exploration for this chapter, we learn to empty our hearts of our stories so we stay in command of our energy. We will create a reservoir of power in our hearts to help finance our best strategies.

We will discuss specific steps to lose our toxic self-importance as a chosen strategy, not because we feel victimized. *So, how are you going to survive? How will you overcome the challenge while bringing out the best and highest within you?* As already discussed, we will begin by reducing emotionality. The best way to eliminate negative emotions is to silence our internal dialogue, and the quickest way to quiet mind chatter is to anchor our locus of awareness in our bodies as we have been practicing (for reference: my first book also discusses more nuances of that process). *A Course in Miracles* notes, "*We don't get angry at facts, but our interpretation of facts.*" The stories we tell ourselves in our heads make us calm or angry. During the mind-body exploration for this chapter, we will practice anchoring our awareness in our heart center, and emptying ourselves of our internal stories.

Now, I recognize you may need more time to be ready to

stop retelling your story. Horrible people do heinous things. I am sure your story could be better. I am sure you are suffering injustices. We see it every day if we watch the news. I am not minimizing this dreadful truth. I don't want to discount your suffering or anyone else. If there were a *Book of Wrong*, in my belief system, some behaviors would be on the first page. This life is brutal. In the mind-body exploration for this chapter, we will move into acceptance of these injustices so we stop wasting energy resisting them. Don't worry; I won't even ask you to take the common compassionate spiritual approach that says, "*Hurt people hurt people*" to try to move you toward forgiveness. This is not that book (that is my other book! LOL!) People do unspeakable acts, so my question in this book is, "*What will you do about it?*"

Unfortunately, we must admit that we can do nothing about many situations. We can't control the world. People don't always listen to us. We have limited resources to address inequities. We are powerless in many ways. I know this is not a fun fact to face. However, I am addressing this gap in human nature head-on that people, especially in the human potential or spiritual movements, rarely want to discuss; we want to feel that we can overcome any obstacle, manifest any outcome, and live among miracles. How is that working for you? Not well, I know. However, you may discover the crux of injustice is a perfectly crafted nexus point to realize the power of knowing how to manage your subtle energies to heighten your consciousness. Through this doorway of our vulnerability, we can learn a skill to invite the power of Loving Intelligence to heal us permanently!

In the mind-body exploration of this chapter, we will find the place of hurt in our hearts and invite the loving, pure light of the Divine to cleanse the area. We will practice releasing our hurt into the light and notice how different we feel afterward. This process works because our emotions fluctuate with our energy field. When our energy is dense and stale, we get stuck in depression. We don't get stuck in our negative stories when our energy is flowing and vibrant. You see, many people think they are depressed, however, their energy is just stale and contracted. Several research studies have been performed documenting how practicing Qigong or Tai Chi contribute to lifting long term depression.

As we start embracing that we are subtle energy power-houses, not just lumps of physical matter, mood fluctuations become far less mysterious. As an energy-sensitive person, emotions are very binary to me. I am not very concerned with my emotions because my primary concern is whether the energy field is expanded or contracted. After years of "stretching" my field open, I stay expanded most of the time, so if I feel dull, I know I need to do some energy rearranging and I will feel fabulous again. Although there may be many layers to remove, the mind-body explorations will eventually heal your energy field while facing harsh truths. You won't feel such twisting inside when you feel violated by an injustice that you can't avoid. You will retain the wisdom of the experience without the gut punch. You will learn how to feel more whole through the injustices you face. I am passionate about teaching people this level of emotional healing is possible and available to all of us, especially if we are skilled.

Advanced spiritual practices help reconcile our power-lessness by shifting our identity. They invite us to transfer our identity from our temporal 3D self to our eternal self, which also inspires us to look at the people in our lives from a much broader and more humble perspective. From this vantage point, we realize we don't know the whole story of anything or anyone. We are all mysteries to each other.

As we shift our identities to our eternal selves, we discover we experience a resilience that our fickle 3D self just can't comprehend. You may be saying, "*I don't want to shift my identity to my eternal self. I want to stay in this 3D world and demand 3D results.*" Again, I hear you. I *totally* understand. Why accept heavenly benefits when we really want earthly ones? It seems like a bad trade! However, your sticky situation may be emerging to beckon you to think bigger. Source Energy is asking you to step up into your greater power, which paradoxically means the little self often needs to be stifled so you can "trade up."

We continue with *A Course In Miracles*, to address this harsh truth. "*To heal, it thus becomes essential for the teacher of God (the spiritual person) to let all his mistakes be corrected. If he senses even the faintest hint of irritation in himself as he responds to anyone, let him instantly realize that he has made an interpretation that is not true, and then let him turn within to his eternal guide and let him judge what the response should be.*" Ouch!!! A tall order, I know! Especially when we are certain we are right! You may be 100% right, but unfortunately, that does not often matter. We may occasionally be asked to eat this type of humble pie. Everything in your body will not want to consent, but you finally reluctantly admit that coming to terms with accepting your powerlessness in that situation is what brings you the greatest peace. We choose to accept our powerlessness to eliminate negativity, and so we can stay in command of our Spirit, which garners our power. To succinctly summarize: *We paradoxically accept our limitations to harness our greatest power.*

I worked with one group for six and a half years,

cleaning our energy fields together. Because they were such intrepid consciousness explorers, I would invite them to do deep healing work that most spiritual centers won't approach. I could ask them to work deeply because we had cultivated the ability to swim in all aspects of our consciousness, including diving into our shadow sides and adroitly returning to lighter ground. We could be fearless emotional explorers of our darker nature because we were skillful at eventually landing in our infinite loving nature.

During those six and a half years, I had a fluctuating fascination with powerlessness. I even offered an evening presentation on powerlessness to the NUMINOUS crowd one night, but no one showed up! LOL! I should have guessed! Who wants to hear about powerlessness? That is not fun. It is demoralizing. However, my advanced Consciousness Athlete group had trust in me and our work together, so they were willing to explore and play with me. We all learned something compelling through our shared experiences. We would consider an area of our lives where we felt powerless and scan our bodies to determine where we hemorrhaged energy to the situation. During the mind-body exploration for that month, we stopped fighting our powerlessness and dove into the predicament. We allowed ourselves to acknowledge what we did not want to accept. We went to the hole within ourselves and sat there... and waited...

We all reported the same phenomenon. When we allowed ourselves to "be with" our powerlessness, we could sense an energetic power emerge through the "hole" in our energy field. It filled in with a loving, healing presence. We found we were at much greater peace within ourselves, which resulted in discovering a surprisingly delightful freedom on the other side! Based on this knowledge, you may want to ask yourself: *What are you fighting that would create greater peace in your life if you skillfully stopped resisting?*

Life sends us humiliating situations daily. Do we want to ride all those emotional roller coasters? It is not very satisfying. Eventually, we see the futility of resisting. *So, how do we face our losses and still feel empowered?* This can only be accomplished through healing our energy fields, which the mind-body explorations aim to achieve.

The first step in the process is catching ourselves when we find that we are in a victimized mental pattern. Then, we mute our mind's chatter by anchoring our awareness in the body and opening up to the Loving Intelligence that connects us all. We realize that Loving Intelligence regards your petty tyrant with the same respect that it regards you and the rest of your life. Through this understanding, we learn to honor the petty tyrant presence in our lives. We set an intention for our higher selves to reveal an appropriate behavioral response. Then we wait and listen. We pause while not mentally being congested with pride or flooded by mind chatter. We use the least emotional energy possible as we ask intricate questions while inviting wisdom to emerge. *How am I going to use resources well? How will I make it through this challenging situation while honoring myself and thriving to the best of my ability? How do I not waste my energy mentally villainizing and proselytizing the horrors of my petty tyrant?*

I realize this process may sound like a stretch, to go from demoralizing situations where we feel powerless to experiencing the satisfaction of a greater inner freedom; however, as we practice the mind-body explorations to pull our Spirit back from unhealthy investments and reinsert our energy back into our energy fields, we are delighted to experience the integrity of this work. Nothing has changed in our outer world, but our inner world is rewired. Words can't describe this inner shift toward integrity. However, we do know we feel a stark contrast and instantly know we don't want to go back!

When I feel that life is challenging me in unexpected ways and my Spirit wanes, I am considerably quicker at calling my energy back, reinserting it into my soul pole, and simultaneously honoring the person or situation I am facing. There is a moment as I am adjusting my field where I can hesitate. I feel like the average David facing the giant Goliath. But that moment of decision to hold my energy tall in the face of obstacles changes my trajectory entirely. After years of honing such skills, I immensely trust this process. Where my energy field felt contracted by a breach, suddenly it feels integrous and whole, even though my outer world circumstances have not changed. I have the resources to face any challenge. My dignity and integrity swell, and I am in a more resourceful mode to address the situation with the highest and best within me.

Most people don't have experience working at these levels of their energy fields, so many of you won't know from whence I speak *yet!* However, because I have been an observer of the mind-body connection for so many years, I would place money on the fact that you already feel stronger after just reading about this process, which means you have pivoted toward mending this relationship challenge. This shift in feeling is only the beginning. If you practice the mind-body explorations, you will have your own trust in this process. I hope you enjoy the discovery as I have.

Let me try again to explain this process energetically because how our subtle energies are invested shapes the quality of our lives. Over the years, I have learned that it is best to share etheric information in different ways so that it is easier to grasp.

You are born with a certain amount of "natal chi" or life force. In addition, each day, after sleeping and eating, you are granted more life force. How you invest your life force determines the quality of your life. Like any other investment, you will lose if you don't choose worthy opportunities. Eventually, you may even have a credit energetic deficit if you mismanage your energy. This energy loss can cause us to become cranky, miserable, demoralized, or _______ (fill in your favorite disempowering emotion.)

The definition of a petty tyrant is that they hold some power over you which can drain your energy. As we have already discussed, it is best to run from them as fast as possible, but there are infinite examples where we can't. In these situations, we have to find a way to minimize our losses or "eat it," so to speak. One choice is to drown ourselves in sorrow, which is not a bad option for a fresh loss. It is wise for us to process our grieving fully. However, there comes a time when grieving becomes self-pity, and this is where we get stuck, often with substances. If we get stuck in melancholy for too long, maybe even making our situation worse with substance addictions, we miss out on powerful growth opportunities.

Most people don't know that if a loss is processed correctly, you can become happier than you were before the loss. This process is referred to in psychology as Post-traumatic Growth, and it involves the positive psychological changes experienced as a result of struggling with highly formidable and complex life circumstances. These adaptive personal changes often only occur when individuals confront significant challenges in their understanding of the world and their place in it. Although it is painful, seismic shifts in thinking and relating to the world and the self are required for post-traumatic growth to occur. This shift in perception contributes to a personal process of deep, meaningful, permanent change. Post-traumatic Growth is a best-kept secret, I know! Who knew loss can often lead to happiness!? Well, I did because I know how the energy field can heal from loss, and I am living proof of this process.

I could roll with this process relatively quickly compared to many because I have a profound sense of my energy field. I identify more with my energy field (my eternal self) and less my body (my temporal self). When I change my energy field, I change how I feel. I always remember that when my energy is contracted, it is not the truth of who I am. It is the "little" me. When I felt energy bleeding out of me as I endured my shamanic dismemberment processes, I always remembered that that resulting weakness was not the "truth" of me. Because I was aware of my energy hemorrhaging, I knew that was the cause of my misery. I could "plug the holes" to stop the energetic bleeding.

I am much more discerning about where I invest my spirit energy now, and I often send out small energy test jaunts to determine if opportunities will weaken or nourish me. I do this by viewing myself in the situation while checking in with my body to decide whether I feel stronger or weaker as I observe myself participating. If I feel conflicting emotions, I honor and explore all of the conflicts.

Another way to think about this process is how Tai Chi masters work. Their hands always gather chi before they release it, and they only release the energy in a measured way so as not to squander it. The more energy we garner, the more energy we have to finance our health, and experience the high-energy emotions of love, joy, and serenity. As we become wise about managing our life force, we realize energy is the real commerce of life, not money.

One of the best ways to determine how well we invest our energy is to determine the energetic qualities of our hearts. Shamans strive to keep their hearts so free and complete that they can laugh during dangerous times.

Don Juan often mentioned how important humor is in the shamanic tradition. They even gave silly names to different levels of petty tyrants, including "jumbo" and "teensy-weensy petty tyrants." Eventually, shamans see right through the ridiculousness of the petty tyrant game and make it a goal to deal with them with a light heart. Humorist Karl Wiggins eloquently connects all of the components I have been sharing with you as he associates laughter with shamanism through the image of a court jester, *"The laughing, joking court jester, who is in reality a Shaman, has all the respect of a king, for there has always been an element of danger lurking about beneath the surface of his smile."* That quote includes everything we contend with in petty tyrant training: threat, detachment, respect, and humor. In the mind-body exploration for this chapter, we will learn how to call back our spirits so that, eventually, we are detached enough to even consider having humor for ourselves as we review our circumstances.

In summary, the role of the petty tyrant is to offer us an opportunity to deconstruct our psyches in a manner that a nice person can't! LOL. Petty tyrants dissect us in some way, like a magnifying glass, showing us the portions of ourselves that are a little too arrogant, a little bit too self-involved, and a little bit too neurotic. By mirroring these flaws back to ourselves, we can examine them with detachment so they can be purified. After we master our petty tyrant situation, we are "put back together" in such a manner that we are so strong and solid that no one will ever deconstruct us in that manner ever again. Your remaining self-importance becomes transferred into straight power.

You have taken a stark comprehensive energetic inventory of yourself, so you will no longer be able to be swayed by flattery, manipulations, or external circumstances that could hurt you. Every choice is between an energetic conservation strategy versus a squandering of emotional energy. If we are to hold such atomic power as spiritual people, it is best we are purified first, and petty tyrants are invaluable to our purification process.

Petty tyrants help us cleanse ourselves. Because we're no longer energetically financing our pride, our energy can be utilized for more successful endeavors, including communicating with a wisdom far greater than ourselves. It is like you have to believe in your power to know you can change the situation, but the humility to know that it is not just you doing the changing. You are in a process more significant than yourself or your petty tyrant. A more pervasive power is orchestrating the dance between the two of you. In the end, you realize it was not the small egoic you that stimulated the alchemy of your transformation but a far grander intelligence. Your petty tyrant generated the perfect storm to reveal your weaknesses so you could call a portion of your spiritual power back that you didn't even know was missing. You may even find yourself smitten with the process once you finally realize this specific chain of people and events facilitated your growth with *precision* (this could be years later).

What is our ultimate goal? To learn how to hold this

world lightly, with non-interference, allowing something more significant to come through you as you lightly facilitate your life. The warrior stance is that of light agility and impeccability with one's energy. According to Don Juan, impeccability is one of the first concerns of warriors because it frees the energy required to face the unknown with our shoulders down and heads up.

We will close this chapter with finishing to the story of Don Juan as he returns to the estate while eliminating his self-importance to conserve the energy he needs to survive. Unfettered by emotions, he scrutinized his petty tyrant. He studied his supervisor's behavior, activities, patterns, and pride. He observed what his supervisor was afraid of and what caused him to rage. He also studied how his manager related with everyone in the house, including the estate owner.

Simultaneously, Don Juan studied himself, including his own fear and pride. He stalked his own emotions as he interacted with this dangerous man. As he studied all of these variables, he measured his behavior accordingly. He became impeccable with his own energy so he could use it to escape at any time. He remained resourceful in the unknown. In the end, because he had studied the various factors so well, Don Juan consciously tweaked a common daily conversation which caused his supervisor to rage so much that he chased Don Juan into the horses' stalls. Don Juan knew the barn well and hid from the horses who became startled. The horses fatally kicked and stamped on the supervisor, who died. Don Juan walked out a free man with no encumbrances.

Notice how, in this story, Don Juan did not kill his supervisor. He merely introduced a pointed conversation with the lady of the house in front of his supervisor. The conversation roused the wrath of the supervisor, which triggered the man's temper that caused him to chase Don Juan into the barn. It was the supervisor's own foibles that enabled Don Juan's escape. In this case, his rage. The situation took care of the man, not Don Juan.

I need to put a very fine tip on this point. The goal is not for our ego to win by putting our petty tyrant in "his place" or giving him his "just due." *Our goal is to gain mastery over our ego and become impeccable with our energy by coming into command of our own humble power, NOT to hold power over others*. This story is about Don Juan coming to a grand understanding of his own power and how to cultivate the humility required to work with greater intelligence for his escape. The end goal of all of his training, and for any shaman, is to garner a bank of power that can be used to finance an extraordinary life and move about challenges with ease.

Another teachable point is that Don Juan could walk out alive because he had the detachment to see his situation clearly without overlaying a victim's story. It appears that Don Juan's courage also ended the sure death of other migrant workers. This exemplifies another aspect of our work together. Eventually, we realize we are called to gather power through the petty tyrant process not just for ourselves *but to be of greater service to others.*

Through this process, we need to cultivate enough humility to admit to ourselves that we do not know what is best. We may need to fight the urge to blanket the situation with specific prayers and intentions. In complex situations, it is often best to intend for the highest and best to emerge for all concerned because there are too many unknown variables. Humility keeps us teachable, which makes us more amenable to allowing higher wisdom to emerge. Our complicated situations did not arise from surface issues, so we often need to marinate in the unknown to allow subtle influential themes to come to the surface.

Sitting in the unknown often feels demoralizing, and it is easy to fall into discouragement. However, if we understand the Higher Consciousness Spiritual Law curriculum, we have a incredibly helpful context to learn from our suffering. From this viewpoint, we accept life's challenges with dignity and do not hemorrhage our energy on arrogance or victimhood by telling ourselves stories that don't serve us. We plug power leaks as we learn to master our emotions when life appears "out of control." We also learn to remain poised in a teachable position, so that we can glean the most learning from any situation.

Incidentally, facing a petty tyrant prepares you to face uncertainties of any unknown because they do not work within accountable boundaries. There is nothing they won't do (more on this in the next chapter). They don't have boundaries to their integrity, so they are great representatives of the unknown. How can we live with dignity, honor, and courage while facing the unknown? Facing a petty tyrant helps us answer that question. So, it's this understanding that if you can deal with a petty tyrant with great skill, you can face the unknown with honor. With your shoulders back and head held high, you can say, "*I have no idea what life will send my way, but I know I can hold my power. I have the skills to navigate any storm because I have emerged victoriously through this highly complex situation that inspired me to face and overcome my weaknesses.*"

After emerging from petty tyrant training, we recognize

that a greater hand orchestrated our instruction with precision, helping us conquer our lower natures and step into our more significant power. As spiritual beings, this includes embracing our eternal nature and being connected to a loving intelligence that connects us all. We were called to this relationship to heal our souls. The courage, bravery, and integrity gained through the petty tyrant curriculum even helped to give us the gift of learning how to face our biggest unknown in this life with honor: our own death.

In the mind-body exploration for this chapter, we will continue to come into command of our awareness by gathering so much power in our lower tan tien that it overflows into our hearts. According to Taoist philosophy, there is a vertical power current of energy in the body, referred to as the taiji pole, and traveling along it is a pulsating field of iridescent white light, creating an energetic field that is so strong that it allows the physical incarnation of our consciousness to take place.

Internationally known author and healer, Barbara Brennan made this ancient eastern approach more available to Westerners when she called this pole the "line of intention" in her book *Light Emerging*. Simply put, Buddhist philosophy suggests that our soul is located in our vertical power current. Regardless of which discipline is used to refer to this place in the body, or how it relates to other subtle energy dimensions, working with our tai chi pole has undeniable palpable effects. Throughout this book, we will learn how to clear our taiji pole, which I also refer to as the "soul pole," to create dramatic shifts within us. When we feel our Spirit wanting to hemorrhage to difficult circumstances, we call it back to the tan tien and then invite the upward current of energy to clear our hearts. I will add to this discussion as we move up the pole in future mind-body explorations.

We will invite the white iridescent and pearlescent light to remove our heart walls toward this person. Heart walls are blocks of dense energy barricading our heart's free flow of energies, generating negative mind chatter. Our heart walls cause us to vacate our hearts and identify with the egoic stories we tell ourselves. We will discipline ourselves to release these stories by cultivating a teachable heart. This will take enormous courage for many of you.

Understand that I am not asking you to face your petty tyrant without defense; I am inviting you to practice becoming more anchored within your soul pole so that when you do encounter this person in real life, you will have established the discipline of staying in command of your power in their presence.

In the mind-body exploration, I invite you to hold awareness in the heart station of your soul pole as you imagine standing in front of your petty tyrant, feeling neutral, unattached to the outcome, and exceedingly safe. We will acknowledge our powerlessness. As we empty ourselves of our temporal stories, we allow the grace of a more wise, detached intelligence to emerge.

We will know we are changing our patterns with our petty tyrant when any clutching, gripping, or grasping in the body reduces, signifying you are no longer hemorrhaging your power. You may also start reviewing the situation from different perspectives, revealing aspects of the relationship you have never noticed because it was eclipsed by your mind chatter. It is delightful to realize how calming it can feel to be less enamored with ourselves so a greater wisdom can emerge. We can be confident we are gathering our power successfully if we suddenly feel the urge to smile as we review our situation.

We will stalk our power in this mind-body exploration by observing the energy surrounding our hearts. When we notice that our energy is "curving in on itself," creating a heart wall, we will know we are starting to turn on ourselves or the other. Our goal is to stop that process in its tracks. Be patient with yourself! If you have been ensnared in negative stories for a while, you may have to break this pattern hundreds of times before establishing the peace you desire. I invite you to maintain a neutral heart that holds dignity and respect for you and your tyrant. We strive for an open heart so big it can hold both of you with great love and deep respect.

One caveat: don't hold yourself accountable for your transformation. Your job is only to offer your sincere willingness be transformed; Infinite Love will do the rest. Just do what you can to open your heart. This process does not call upon weak, sappy hallmark card love but the transcendent relentless frequency of eternal love. We do this to recognize the mutual honor of being summoned into each other's life as noble teachers. As *A Course In Miracles* states, our only job is merely to have the sincere and earnest *"willingness"* to *"begin the miracle."* Infinite Love will do the rest!

I will stop writing now because it is time for you to go into yourself and mine your own learning. Nothing will take the place of doing these mind-body explorations because they are designed to help you find your way into noble wise places within yourself. If a solution could have been located outside of yourself, you would have found it by now! It is time to go within. There are no books for what you are facing. There is no cheap grace. The answers you need now can only be found by getting quiet within yourself to allow an intelligence greater than your smaller self to emerge.

Buddha used a word to describe his state of consciousness after his enlightenment; it was tathagata, a word often translated as "one who has gone." Buddha described himself as having rid himself of his lower egoic nature by stating his old self was "gone." Understand that when we learn to anchor in our hearts and stop being enamored with our stories, we rest in our more significant nature: love. Our lower selves are "gone," so we can be of better vessel for service to others. I encourage you to start enjoying being "gone" from your egoic self to rest in higher love and savor its peace. The mind-body exploration will offer you the skills to find this peace through authentic acceptance and learn how to stay there for extended periods. Set your bar high. Even consider seeking to smile as you endure. Enjoy.

You can find the mind-body exploration audio,
Healing Hearts at
NuminousOnline.org/pearl
Enter the password: pearl

3

SEEING CLEARLY

Do you walk away from a conversation with your tyrant
friend and still have more questions than answers?
Do you notice that your tyrant's actions
don't match his/her words?
Do you often wonder why you feel uneasy
around this person?
Do you let yourself acknowledge you
have these questions?

The last chapter discussed maintaining an empowered stance with an open, neutral heart as you face complex challenges. You may need to call upon your ability to remain neutral as we explore this book's most difficult topics in this chapter. I invite you to maintain a sovereign perspective because we will discuss some pretty gritty stuff that is often inappropriate for "polite people." This information will challenge spiritual people like me, who love to love, laugh, and feel sweetness.

Because of my strong leanings into light, I was particularly resistant to these truths. I do not enjoy drama. I watch virtually no television series or movies because I don't even like investing my spirit in fake dramas. Dramas bore me. However, due to a series of events, Source Energy seemed to go out of its way to teach me about this "dramatic" segment of human nature: petty tyrants. I was only released from my rigorous training when I could write this curriculum on how spiritual people can interact with them successfully.

It has taken me fifteen years to assimilate this information, and I have just now sat down to write this book because I did not want to revisit this energy. During that time, people wrestling with petty tyrants would cross my path, and I would teach them how to navigate their troubling waters. They sincerely appreciated my approach. I knew I had been given a high teaching because of the gratitude people showed for this work. However, I was reluctant to bring it to the public. Because we live in such uncertain times, I finally felt it was time to put my spiritual approach to petty tyrant training into book form to help others.

This chapter may be challenging to read as a spiritual person, so I am pausing for a moment to honor your sensitivities. In the last chapter, we discussed being called to stay awake at the wheel while cultivating discernment. We should not assume that we know better or that "love will solve it all." We are to remain empty of our egoic selves to always be teachable. I am reminded of a passage in *A Course In Miracles*. "*Trust not your good intentions. They are not enough. But trust implicitly your willingness, whatever else may enter. Concentrate only on this, and be not disturbed that shadows surround it.*" I have come to trust these words. My small egoic self does not know what is best in any situation, but I do know that if I am willing to be an instrument of healing for all concerned without being attached to a specific outcome, I will be successful at being an instrument of peace for myself and others.

M. Scott Peck, author of *The Road Less Traveled,* which was on the NY Times Best Sellers list for over ten years, validated this approach when he answered a question posed by an audience participant. *"How do I know I am doing the right thing?"* Dr. Peck responded that the question was the single most common question he was asked, and then he answered, *"There is no such formula. The unconscious is always one step ahead of the conscious mind—the one that knows things—so it's impossible to know for sure. But if you're willing to sit with ambiguity, to accept uncertainties and contradictory meanings, then your unconscious will always be a step ahead of your conscious mind in the right direction. You will, therefore, do the right thing, though you won't know it now."* I also heard Dr. Peck address this topic concerning responding to uncertainty. He suggested that if we had a willingness to do the right thing that *"you will do the right thing, even if you don't have the luxury of knowing it at the time."* At this point in our journey of being an advanced spiritual adherent, we need to be content with our willingness to be an instrument of healing for all (even though we don't know what that means in complex situations) so our unconscious mind can lead our conscious minds in the right direction during our periods of uncertainty.

We can not be effective if we proceed to be full of ourselves. Don't think you know the "perfect outcome" for the situation; I guarantee you, you don't. The petty tyrant relationship is highly correlated with the trickster archetype, meaning hidden knowledge will be judiciously revealed, giving your story many twists and turns and revealing deep knowledge before it ends. However, if we follow the petty tyrant curriculum through this mysterious process, we will learn how to become humble enough to effectively co-create with Infinite Love, generating joy.

A Course In Miracles addresses this delicate balance in this passage, *"Humility will never ask you to be content with littleness. But it does require that you be not content with less than greatness that comes not of you."* Are you starting to see the paradox? We are not becoming humble so that we feel like specks of dirt. We become humble (you could say small) to experience substantial wisdom far more significant than our limited egos would allow. There is no room for Infinite Intelligent wisdom revelations when we are full of what we think we know, how we believe things should roll, or what we presume others should do. When we learn to move our egos out of the way, we can experience spontaneous grace. As we approach these dicey topics, I ask you to fall back into the neutral space you cultivated in your mind-body-heart meditation in the last chapter so you can receive the new information in this chapter with a spacious heart. If we are attentive, we may notice an extraordinary alchemy occurring.

Remember we defined "jumbo" petty tyrants between 8 and 10 on our friend-to-tyrant scale? We will explore the personality types at this most extreme position on this spectrum. There is an informative book on a similar subject written by Dr. Martha Stout, author of *The Sociopath Next Door,* in which she presents startling statistics. She notes that 4% of the population qualifies as being sociopaths, which is defined as someone who doesn't have a conscience. These people have no concern over right or wrong, and their brains demonstrate this indifference.

When scientists look at the brains of sociopaths, they're significantly different than the rest of the population. The portion of the brain that helps healthy people feel emotions like love, sweetness, kindness, and empathy does not function in sociopaths. Due to limbic system malfunction, one out of twenty-five people, if their brains were scanned, would qualify to be a sociopath. Take a moment to let that statistic sink in. If you live in a neighborhood of sorts, it will take you only a short time to think of twenty-five people who live relatively close to you. Statistically speaking, one of those people qualifies to be sociopathic.

Obviously, this does not mean that every sociopath has dead bodies in their basement. Many of them blend well into society without exhibiting such behavior because they don't want to be bothered with brushes with the law. However, if push came to shove, understand that 4% of the population would have zero problems pulling a trigger. This may be a startling statistic and could rattle you a bit. If so, I am sorry for your discomfort. However, I believe more people must address this sad truth. Because this is a high percentage of people, we must humble ourselves and face the reality they live among us.

The brains of sociopaths differ significantly from the rest of the 96% of the population because of their deficiencies in the neocortex and the primitive limbic system, which deals with emotion and socialization. These brain deficits cause sociopaths to callously nonchalantly respond to violence, and tragedy, unlike the rest of the population. In tests designed to measure psychological reactivity, sociopaths distinctly flatline, exhibiting no emotionality despite viewing tragic graphic scenes. For instance, they may experience the same biological response to a bloody car wreck that they would experience while viewing a picture of a set of teacups.

Sociopaths don't have the emotional life of somebody who has what I call a "normal emotional pallet." At the beginning of her book, Dr. Stout goes to great lengths to coax ordinary people to insert themselves into the emotionally deficient brains of sociopaths. She has to work very hard, bending our brains to consider their perspective because emotionally ordinary people intuitively rebel against such darkness. We don't want to think that the brains of others, often people we know and love, are so significantly emotionally deficient that they are essentially inhumane relative to the twenty-four people surrounding them.

Stout also states how their brains resist psychological or medical treatment. In general, they are not capable of rehabilitation because their deficits are neurological, not psychological. I remember when I came to understand that the sociopathic brain was different than mine. It was actually a relief to me. Instead of ruminating about their harsh behaviors, I could finally move toward 100% acceptance. I knew there was nothing I could do to change the other person. Paradoxically, this enabled me to sink into greater forgiveness for them while raising my awareness to be more vigilant in all areas of my life.

For instance, years ago, there was a woman on our local news who drowned her own four children in her bathtub. I remember recoiling in horror as I joined conversations when people would say, *"Oh my God! How could a mother do that to her kids?"* Now, I hear stories like that and say, "Yup, just another sociopath," and move on. Since I realized that most people who make the news due to their appalling behavior perform such outrageous acts because their brains are different, it is far easier for me to "let it go" when I hear these stories. I have learned to watch out for myself more, but I stopped experiencing moral outrage at individuals; however, now I am observing petty tyrant signature behaviors in organizations, which is another level of training I am currently observing. This knowledge certainly changes how you view people in power.

Understand that the mother could easily drown her children because her kids were not her kids to her; they were objects. Her children were only pawns in her game of life, not living human beings with wide-ranging emotional pallets. It is essential for you to understand this distinction. Sociopaths look at people around them as pawns for entertainment because, essentially, they are bored. They live in the executive functioning portion of their brains, so their emotional centers are deadened. They are problem solvers, not lovers. Any behaviors that appear to originate from emotion are the sociopath mimicking normal emotions to blend their behavior with others so as not to suffer consequences of interference with their goals. It is well known that sociopaths study emotionally healthy people like prey, as they watch for feeling patterns in others. Experts surmise they experience such a startling vacuous daily emptiness that they know they are different from us. They become "actors and actresses" as they strive to appear like the rest of society so their contrary motives are not discovered.

Stout starkly contrasts what entertains sociopaths versus emotionally healthy people. Each day, we perform a multitude of repetitive mundane activities. For instance, we take the same drive to work every day, shovel the same driveway, or sweep the same floors. When we perform hours and hours of tedious, mundane activities, we entertain ourselves by sifting through our emotional lives. We relive conversations, evaluate different responses, and consider emotional nuance in future interactions. As we sift through our emotionally dynamic landscapes, we sit at traffic lights and are entertained.

A sociopath whose limbic system isn't working doesn't experience emotional entertainment, so they are bored beyond belief with the mundane tasks of life. Because not much is happening inside them emotionally, they enjoy manipulating things and people outside themselves like pawns on a game board for entertainment. Unfortunately, innocent people often become the game pieces they like to control for entertainment. Watching us must sometimes be more entertaining than watching a movie.

If you resist this information, please think about the last chapter. Our desire for goodness makes us repel thoughts of such darkness, so I must stress remaining teachable. We must understand that not only are their brains distinctly different, but even their whole bodies are different. Their skin can literally be cold to the touch. They don't jump if they have been startled. A sociopath can't even sweat or show nervousness.

Sociopaths thrive in fields where most of us would crash and burn, such as stunt movie performers or international espionage. I heard a sociopath say once, "*Everything is easier for a sociopath.*" This makes perfect sense! Think about how tentative you were in high school as you learned about yourself within a more mature social order. Can you imagine if you had zero fear back then? How different would your high school career have been without that anxiety? Sociopaths often reveal themselves through excessive risk-taking, fearlessness, shamelessness, and impulsive actions. Being bored is their hallmark. Many scientists believe their reckless behavior results from an unfathomable emotional vacuity and emptiness, so risk-taking helps them feel alive.

In spiritual circles, we are taught that *"Everybody is the same. We are all God's children. Be one hundred percent tolerant. We're all equal."* Anyone who dares to say anything else is vilified and shamed, yet this response is blatant, dangerous ignorance. Do you see the conflict setting into this discussion? Do you see how controversial this topic is within spiritual circles, which is why I did not want to bother writing this book for so many years? Twenty-four people would not want to shoot you even if you were hurting their family. However, one out of 25 people would have no problem pulling the trigger to end your life and nonchalantly eat an ice cream ten minutes later with your blood on their hands. We must come to terms with this truth. Spirituality tells us that we are all God's children. I still agree with that; however, if some of God's children have no problem killing for entertainment, then a greater level of discernment is called for from the rest of God's children, especially if they are "spiritual"...*Yes???* (you may want to nod your head up and down to let that land within you if you resist these statistics.)

Ironically, I believe that sociopaths have incarnated for the greater good of all of us. When I heard that 4% of us are sociopathic, for some reason, I said to myself, *"That is no accident"* because it seemed like such an intentional percentage. What if the human race is a delicate blend of sound, neutral, and evil, and a specific recipe is required to perform our purposes here? What if we need the contrasts of each to glean arcane wisdom while we play the game of "Divine Wake Up"?

Eventually, many of us evolve to recognize that we are all

worthy in the eyes of Infinite Love. However, it is advisable that spiritual adherents become more discerning and acknowledge that the twenty-fifth person in line should be treated differently than the other twenty-four people. Universally applying spiritual tenets is not just inappropriate, it is dangerous. Sociopaths prey on those of us who strive to live spiritual values such as tolerance, interconnection, love, and care, because our ideals can easily be used to manipulate us.

It is incredibly unfair, but those of us who are spiritual often end up inadvertently enabling sociopaths. I have witnessed spiritual leaders, again and again, draw formidable petty tyrants into their lives. People of great light can attract those of incredible darkness. I remember Marianne Williamson saying years ago that *sometimes it's not our darkness that draws other's darkness but our light.* Shining our light indiscriminately because we think we know what is "good" without running it by Source Energy for discernment sets us up to be non-primary characters in sociopaths' virtual reality games. Our light and desire to love are easily manipulated and used against us to put ourselves and others in risky situations with people with zero regard for our safety.

I will end this part of the discussion on a more positive note. Dr. Stout also writes that 96% of people who go to war have a tendency to either purposely misfire when expected to shoot a gun or delay firing until their superior is watching. The majority of people are good people. Many strangers would even take a bullet for us. Invisible, quiet, and noble beauty is rampant but does not make the evening news.

We will now shift our discussion to move into the neurology of narcissism and how it relates to people at the 8-10 portion of our friend-to-tyrant scale. Then, I will swing back and discuss how we, as spiritual people, have our unique blend of narcissism (our projections onto others without considering their true orientations), which is what gets us into trouble in the first place!

In *The Sociopath Next Door*, Dr. Stout said, metaphorically speaking, half of a sociopath would be a narcissist. A narcissist, according to research, is someone who has absolutely no empathy. Their entire world revolves around them. Narcissistic personality disorder is a mental health condition in which people have an unreasonably high sense of their own importance. They need and seek too much attention and want people to admire them. People with this disorder lack the ability to understand or care about the feelings of others.

Similar to sociopathy, narcism has a neurological origin. Several studies performed have demonstrated narcissists have structural abnormalities in regions of the brain linked to empathy, specifically in the pre-frontal cortex. For narcissists, a portion of their brain responsible for empathy has less gray matter in a part of the cerebral cortex and the left anterior insula, which lessens their ability to generate empathy.

The statistics are higher for narcissists than for sociopaths. Years ago, when I first researched this, it was estimated about 10% of the population was narcissistic; one out of 10 people would be considered a narcissist. Now, I see that current statistics estimate about 6%. After observing this phenomenon for a decade and a half, either way, there is still a significant number of people who demonstrate narcissism, many of whom rise to positions of power. Because of these relatively high percentages, it is wise for us to become educated about this phenomenon. We can feel forgiveness, not frustration, as we recognize their behavior, similar to sociopaths, is neurologically based, not psychologically based.

Narcissists are biologically different than emotionally healthy populations, which means we must deal with them differently as well. When scientists scanned the brains of 34 people, including 17 individuals who had a narcissistic personality disorder, they found that the degree to which a person was able to exhibit empathy was correlated with the volume of grey matter in the cerebral cortex in the left anterior insula. This may be why it doesn't matter how many times or how many ways you explain your perspective on a topic; your narcissist literally *can't* comprehend your viewpoint at all! Usually, people exhaust themselves for years before figuring this out with their local narcissist.

So, let's sit with this for a minute. One out of 25 people are sociopathic because they don't experience emotion, and 2 (1.5 rounded up) out of twenty-five people are narcissistic because they don't experience empathy. We are arriving at a significant portion of the population; twelve out of one hundred or three out of twenty five people have biologically malfunctioning emotional brains, causing substantial problems for the rest of us.

To make matters much worse, due to our societal entitlement culture, many researchers are sounding the alarm that narcissism is on the rise. Ten percent of young people exhibit narcissism personality disordered traits at some point in their lives, versus only three percent in the over sixty-five population. As our young people become more narcissistic, we must become skilled in how to maneuver around these sticky personalities stealthily.

It is critically important for us to empty ourselves of

ourselves to see these people clearly because narcissists can't see us at all! Narcissists acknowledge their feelings only but won't recognize ours. Tragically, spiritual adherents are often so full of their goodwill that they don't even notice their emotions don't exist in the mind of their narcissist tyrant. It is common to find an open-hearted spiritual person who loves a narcissist in their life so much they bend, tolerate, and extend themselves to maintain the relationship. They bob and weave for years before they realize they have received zero authentic reciprocation. Tragically, it is common for the spiritual person to have lost much of their spiritual power in the process. Their identities often become virtually eroded because they've indiscriminately applied beautiful spiritual principles to emotionally vacant people.

There are two books I recommend reading regarding how to deal with narcissists. One is called *Disarming the Narcissist by* Wendy Behary, and the other book is called *The Gaslight Effect* by Dr. Robin Stern. *The Gaslight Effect* is the origin of a popular metaphor now commonly referred to as "gaslighting." Dr Stern used this term to refer to the 1944 movie *Gaslight* with Ingrid Bergman. It was a horror film of the time where the character of Ingrid Bergman, Paula, was befriended by a gentleman soon after her wealthy aunt died. After a two-week whirlwind romance, they marry. Instead of her husband emotionally supporting her, he strives to make Paula feel like she is insane so he can take control of her inheritance.

Her husband does whatever he can to make her doubt herself, including fooling with the gaslight. He starts making the gaslight flicker by turning lights on and off, which reduces the gas to the gaslight, causing it to blink. Paula would ask her husband, "*Did you see the gaslight flicker?*" and he'd essentially say, "*No, I didn't see anything; I don't know what you're talking about.*" In many other ways, he continues to discredit Paula's experiences, which causes her to question her valid thoughts and feelings. He is playing with her mind to get her to question her sanity and make her doubt what she knows is true, including her sense of herself. As time progresses, she starts devolving into a fragile human being.

At the movie's end, an external observer is needed to help Paula validate that the gaslight is indeed flickering, because her husband is in the attic looking for papers to steal. Once Paula gets validation from an external source, she integrates all the information and everything suddenly makes sense. She recognizes that her husband has been manipulating her to access her wealth. The Gaslight Effect is a good metaphor for understanding how a good-natured person striving to meet her spouse's needs can be manipulated by someone appearing to be emotionally attentive.

I recognize this is not fun to discuss and certainly is frowned upon in polite spiritual circles (I have been the object of the glares!) However, spiritual circles are precisely where this complicated topic needs to be acknowledged and confronted when it appears because spiritual people are especially vulnerable to such behavior.

Years ago, a man with a record of sexually assaulting a woman at another spiritual organization was attending another church down the road. His former arrest showed he presented with a different name at each spiritual organization. This man was so bored that he did not even sit for Sunday service; he would roam the halls during church while others were listening to the message. After church, he would often inject himself into positions of prominence in committee meetings. He blatantly demonstrated he did not want to be bothered learning with the community; he just gravitated to adopting leadership positions, enabling him free access to others. His adverse behavior was so crystal clear, and yet, due to a common ignorance in management (most people are just not educated on such deceptive behavior), he was able to continue making many people uncomfortable causing a rift within the church. Management wanted to be loving and tolerant, as all good spiritual organizations strive to be. Because of their spiritual predispositions, they could not "see" his suspicious behavior. He approached me a few times, and I steered as far away as possible, and I stopped attending for a while.

This information can feel repulsive to our emotional orientations because it is not what we want to consider in our spiritual organizations. When we attend spiritual gatherings, we want to hear about peace and love, and sing the Coca-Cola song with these words: " *I would like to teach the whole world to sing in peace and harmony...how wonderful that would be, how beautiful that would be.*" As someone who dedicated herself to peace meditation research by founding the **Resonant Peaceful Cities Project,** I wish more than anyone this information was not true. I believe I was forced to confront this these facts from Source because I could assimilate this intense, intricate information and share it with others in an empowering manner. Intelligent Love had to go to great lengths to remove my hazy spiritual lens so I could clearly see the darker sides of human nature.

To be 100% clear on my orientation to this work, I believe this book is a "high teaching." I say that because it follows infinite energy flows, not earthly knowledge. This work strengthens our energies first and then our minds. It's not the other way around, as most books work. I don't even take credit for the actual curriculum for this work. I have added my life experiences and knowledge to illuminate it. However, I don't even feel like this book is "my work." I am just "reporting the news" regarding something you "might like to know" about how your energy already works.

Eventually, after I had learned the intricacies of the darker sides of human nature, the themes of this book were officially weaved together into a curriculum through what I consider a "download" from higher realms while I was in Brazil over a decade ago. I refer to this work as a Spiritual Law School Curriculum. It is not my curriculum; it is a Juris Doctorate of Earthly Spiritual Law School. Like all curriculums, there is more to learn after the degree, however, I believe, this work, integrates a significant body of knowledge that offers a solid foundation for even more advanced training.

Soon after I received the download, I briefly taught this work publicly. One spiritual leader called the work "Electrifying." Another man confided in me after a presentation, *"Bethany, my wife, and I went to thirty-six counselors, psychiatrists, and clergy, and it was not until tonight that I figured out why my marriage did not work. I wish I had known this information all those years."* This book is a healing salve for our current toxic, divisive culture. I seem to be downloading the post-doc curriculum now.

I have lightly alluded to the fact that, as spiritual people, we have our own brand of narcissism. We can project our agreeableness, goodwill, and open-heartedness onto individuals who have not earned them. Because we are so "full" of our positive intentions, we can't "see" their deficits. In these cases, similar to narcissists, we don't even realize we are not "taking in the other." Our unwillingness to see mental health conditions, combined with our attachments to universal principles, cause us to treat all people the same indiscriminately. We have our successful relationship behavior toolbox, and we assume we need to use the same relationship tools for everyone, but this is untrue. Responding with a "one size fits all" response makes us easy prey for tyrants.

It is astonishing how most people can be so predictably easy to manipulate. However, when our locus of awareness is anchored in our bodies, it is much harder for us to be fooled. As we become more skilled at using our bodies to ensure that our spiritual power is "home with us," we are much more attentive to our environments. Because our energies are not scattered, our spirit is present to notice red flag nuances, making it inconceivable to gloss over our cognitive dissonances, beckoning us to higher truths. Our spirit traversing through the acupuncture meridians of our bodies makes it impossible for us to lie to ourselves or ignore our body's cues, which are trying to keep us safe. The combination of keeping our spirit anchored in our body and our awareness anchored in our open, teachable hearts while maintaining a deep honoring of ourselves makes us far less likely to be duped. Because we have learned to take better inventory of the energies traveling through our bodies, we become more awake at the wheel, alarming us when something is incorrect.

I will give you an example of how an educated spiritual leader who published a book with a well-known publishing company was duped. She was sharing with me how she started dating someone who was putting off signals that he may not be honorable and have problems with substance abuse. She told me how she would watch TV with him. She noticed that he preferred shows that discussed murderers and their strategies for killing people, most often marital partners. (Remember, she is a spiritual author with significant credentials behind her.) Her gut started to click in, so she felt compelled to say to him, *"You know, I get the feeling that you're watching these shows because you want to do that to me someday?"* The man turned to her and chillingly responded, *"Kathy, (not her real name) if I were to do that, I would completely plan it first."* He said the words so coldly that foreboding chills traveled up and down her spine, yet she tried to argue with her body's wisdom for the rest of the night. She kept saying things to herself like, *"Well, you know, he does come from an alcoholic family, and he did take steroids when he was younger, which could have really destroyed his social functioning. I am sure he did not mean what he sounded like."* This is what I mean by how it is our spiritual narcissism that gets us into these problems in the first place!

We ignore how other people present themselves because we feel so sure of our worldview, which is often influenced by the spiritual books we read. Instead of seeing the truth of overt behavior, we substitute plausible explanations based on our own behavior repertoire. Do you understand now why it is essential to become skilled at "emptying" ourselves so that we can truly "see?"

In this situation, the severely alcoholic individual talked about a plan of how he would go about murdering Kathy. She was so full of the spiritual recipes in her own head that she explained away his alarming response by attributing it to his family history and taking steroids. This woman was at the point where she was questioning everything she was so sure she believed in when she said, *"I thought I could heal the world!"* Incidentally, I heard that same exact sentence from another prominent spiritual teacher who thought he could have also "*healed the world*" as he unpacked his former relationship with a narcissist with me. Both teachers are impressive, intelligent, and accomplished people in the spiritual community. They just didn't know what they didn't know and then found themselves engaging in top-level petty tyrant situations.

The same spiritual narcissism is also involved when people in a spiritual community shame others who petty tyrants are tormenting. Ironically, spiritual communities, whether they be Christian, Jewish, Muslim, Buddhist, or New Age, can be severely judgmental. *Have you noticed?* Judgment has a unique stamp of condescension in new-age communities because of the widely accepted belief that we "create our own reality." It is common to be in these communities and be blamed for the neurological shortcomings of your petty tyrant. *"Just ignore it, lift your frequency, don't give it power, and it will disappear."* Here is another example of new age shaming, "*You see this because of all the negativity inside of you, not her!*" You may hear, "*Why do you attract such negative people?*" asked with dripped disdain. I have known too many stellar people of incredible light and integrity be crucified by people without integrity.

I know of a beautiful mental health counselor. Full of love and light. She just loved to love. She dated a man for three months who had two wives that had died. At the end of their relationship, he took her out to the woods and told her that he would have killed her then if the counselor's brother did not know who she was with and where she was. This man made his nefarious intentions clear to the counselor and continued to stalk and threaten her as if he was just waiting for the right opportunity to accomplish his goal. This woman immediately had to leave everything she owned and knew, including her condominium and pets, to disappear underground for two years. She slept on the sofas of others to find refuge from his relentless menacing stalking. The new age community shamed her severely, and yet the most non-spiritual people showed her the most compassion and lovingly extended themselves to teach her how to keep herself safe.

It is common for people to make snap judgments about others' behaviors and pontificate quick solutions while they ignore the obvious cognitive dissonance they are experiencing. One of the most historical examples of this is the healer historically known as Jesus, who was so powerful he changed the face of the globe because people are still talking about him over two thousand years later! His own people crucified him. People did not like him because he broke the Pharisee's rules and became more popular than them. He was healing the "unclean" and partying with the poor and afflicted. So, if the spiritual community is shaming you for your situation, you are in good company. Your beautiful open heart, willingness to be of service, and kindness that you want to extend indiscriminately may draw these quick judgments. Don't let them get to you.

Far more resources are available online regarding these topics than I had access to fifteen years ago. I am no expert on sociopaths and narcissists. I am only a teacher on maintaining our energy as we respond to them. I suggest that if you suspect you are dealing with one of these two types of people, find some quality thought leaders and learn how to navigate your communications with them. However, I can give you some broad brush stroke behaviors to look for that may give you a starting point for your research.

I will list some behaviors here that are considered toxic;

your job is to review the people in your life and ask if they exhibit some of them. Before I begin, though, I want to share with you a story about how I shared these characteristics with a spiritual group, and one woman started agonizing about whether or not she could be a narcissist. That is a classic spiritual person for you. One person in the group said, "*You are obviously not a narcissist or sociopath because if you were, it would not even cause you a second of worry if you were one!*"

I have an observation on this topic after years of observing people in my biofeedback practice. As we have discussed, sociopaths have no conscience, which means they feel zero remorse, so there is nothing they won't do. Conversely, I observe spiritual people who come see me for biofeedback and energy work who could emotionally beat themselves up relentlessly for *possibly* using the wrong tone of voice on the phone! Their conscience is almost so conscious, so hyper-aware, that they are far more anxiety-ridden than the rest of the population.

I believe that this phenomenon is a critical differential to highlight as we recognize how anxiety presents when spiritual consciousness enters, which is why it is common for the most anxious people to be the most spiritual people. Watching this process can be challenging because spiritual people can torment themselves with their awareness. This is a subject for another book, but understand that all of the work I teach leads the body into states that are incompatible with anxiety. Anxiety is primarily a physiological or body response, and secondarily a psychological response. Relying exclusively on talk therapy to alter nervous system anxiety patterns is like trying to move the top of a glacier above water without acknowledging the base under the water.

Until the base is acknowledged, the body in this metaphor, people unnecessarily suffer much longer with anxiety than they ever should. *My goal is always to encourage spiritual people to "rest" within thier bodies to finally get their spirituality to work for them, not against them.* Too many people are tortured by their minds, and drug-pushing organizations are not helping as they are quick to prescribe anti-anxiety medications for a quick fix. However, the honest short answer to reducing anxiety is to anchor their locus of awareness in their bodies. I understand that this requires the significant mental discipline you are learning in this book, which I admit is not easy, so most people prefer to take drugs instead.

As I mention these signs of toxic behavior, I suggest that you keep your awareness anchored in your heart and stay aware of feelings in your body as you read. Remain teachable as you allow your body's wisdom to emerge, which will help you discern whether or not you are observing behaviors associated with someone who could be classified as sociopath or narcissistic. Here are some general red flags of toxic behaviors: excessive need for flattery, self-absorption, thrill-seeking, lack of empathy, humiliation, infidelity, and mocking or discrediting normal emotions.

I remember that, in one of my situations, I read a book on relationships and tried to implement the book's advice by having a constructive conversation with one of my petty tyrants. The person completely mocked me for my efforts. Another red flag of destructive relationship behavior is that it is common for toxic people to resist commonly accepted and well-established healthy interpersonal communication styles.

Another significant red flag signaling you are dealing

with a narcissist or a sociopath is that they exhibit zero accountability. After conversing regarding their responsibilities with my petty tyrants, I often lamented, *"It is like nailing jello to a wall!"* They absolutely refuse to be held to their own promises. These personality disorders can be so slippery that author Wendy Behary warns readers in her book *Disarming the Narcissist* that if you have a narcissist in your life, one of the first things you need to decide is whether or not that person is worth keeping in your life. The only cure for narcissism is accountability, and narcissists will put you through so much hell as you strive to hold them accountable; it will often be the wiser choice to leave immediately. The behaviors I already mentioned are just a few examples of toxic behavior. You should check in with your gut and heart to see if any of these behaviors are more salient to you, and start your research by investigating that behavior.

The metaphor I often use for discussing how narcissists can destroy us as we strive to hold them accountable is the video I have seen of a crocodile with a body in its mouth. You will see the crocodile toss the body left and right and back and forth, maybe even thrashing it on the ground. Its prey will try to escape the crocodile's mouth with all its might. If the crocodile does not choose to consume the body, the body ends up a wounded mess on the ground as the crocodile glides away in the water, unconcerned about the mortal wounds it caused. As I got wise, I often saw this vignette in my mind if I found myself tangling with a petty tyrant. The image warned me not to expend too much energy because the person was obviously playing me, and I meant nothing to them.

I finally realized that petty tyrants don't bend where we would bend, and they don't stop where we would stop.

Because they are not bound by an ounce of integrity, they take you beyond the brink of healthy social norms. A person of healthy integrity will not cross certain lines. However, a narcissist or sociopath crosses over normative social lines daily and won't think twice about it! Understand, if you're trying to hold a sociopath or narcissist accountable, then they are going to be dancing over those lines often, and you will virtually never win. Because they are not bothered with ethics, they have far more behavioral options than you do. I often say do not get into the sandbox with a narcissist or a sociopath; do not play with them. If you start to observe any of these behaviors, the first thing that all experts say to do is run, run, run!

As spiritual people, we can run, run, run with an open heart. We can keep a soft heart as we walk out the door and go in the opposite direction while knowing that loving ourselves is equally important. By honoring our own knowing, seeing the person clearly, and acknowledging toxic behavior, we recognize that the highest form of love in this situation may be to honor ourselves and the other person by walking away. However, the minute you get into their lagoon, the minute you start sparring with them thinking you know better or you are going to "teach him/her a lesson," they will be the crocodile, and you will most often be that body lying on the ground... if you are lucky!

This rule has one exception, and I will mention that now. Dr. Stout documents in her book that by midlife, it is common for sociopaths to take themselves down by their own hand, similar to how Don Juan's supervisor was eliminated by his own uncontrolled rage, not by Don Juan. By that point, it is common for them to have harmed enough people along the way that they left a series of metaphorical dead bodies, or possibly even real dead bodies, in their wake. They develop histories that follow them, and people they have hurt start to gather and compare notes.

Suppose their behavior has been outrageous enough, and they have interfered with enough people of influence over time. In that case, it is common for someone to be called to make that toxic individual accountable, such as taking them to court or convicting them of a crime. However, that person may go through hell in doing so. Even highly skilled mental health care professionals who work with these people regularly tell stories of just how much they need to guard their minds because these people have manipulated their lives. These are highly skilled doctors and therapists who often watch for manipulations. However, they *still* get duped even though they should "know better." So, if experts in the field are getting harmed by these toxic tyrants while *watching* for toxic behaviors, how can innocent, lovely, open-hearted spiritual people respond effectively to them? Unfortunately, most won't stand a chance unless they have educated themselves on this topic. If they see and acknowledge the destructive behavior for what it is and don't project their goodwill onto the person, they won't experience a shred of guilt as they turn on their heel and walk away, hopefully quickly!

I have witnessed people who want to confront a sociopath or narcissist because the toxic individual has bruised their ego. This rarely goes well for the confronting individual. A version of this is when spiritual people believe they can "kill them with kindness" or "show them what it is like to be truly loved." Any time you lead with your ego with these people, it will get handed right back to you only with an egg on it. You will get slimed. Why? Remember, their role is to eliminate our egos. Through Don Juan's story, we learned that petty tyrants are here to be clean, clear mirrors that reflect our excessive self-ingratiating attitudes. Their incredible cunning and understanding of exploiting human weakness is far better than yours. So, it's often just as wise to walk away. Keep your heart open, but walk away before you get too damaged. As we will see in the mind-body exploration for this chapter, be sure to see the behavior *clearly* so you don't feel guilty as you honor yourself walking away.

To put a fine point on this subject before we close, let's talk about the times when we *can't* walk away because this is when spiritual growth accelerates significantly. Part of the official definition of a petty tyrant is that they hold some power over you, and this is especially true when you can't escape because it could be your disabled spouse, your boss at a rare job, or what I believe to be the most difficult of all, your child. I have witnessed narcissistic or sociopathic children who have amazingly spiritually advanced parents, which does not seem to be an accident to me.

If you find yourself in situations where you know you cannot walk away, please take some solace and consider if, on a higher level, you chose to take an accelerated path toward your spiritual evolution. So, take a moment and breathe that understanding deep into your bones. Many people will have a severe petty tyrant in their lives for maybe ten, fifteen, or even twenty years. It is difficult to watch as you see the person struggling with repeated hurtful behavior such as pathological lying, constant stealing, relentless pity seeking, or excessive charming, or sexual behavior. Tyrants could be cruel or even demonstrate sadistic verbal and physical abuse. Imagine dealing with such demoralizing behavior for decades. It is common because these pernicious behaviors can often be so subtle that people don't see the behavior for what it is. They just know they always feel troubled regarding that relationship.

If, after reading this book, you start to acknowledge, *"Wow, I really do have a petty tyrant in my life, and it is someone I can't escape,"* then the first thing I want you to do is remember your tyrant is your best chance for accessing the pearl of heightened consciousness within you. When life is easy, we don't dig that deep to find answers. However, this journey within, if skilled, will enable us to rid ourselves of attachments occluding heightened consciousness. This person will force you to become conscious of choosing between "trading up" or "caving in" on yourself, so you can choose which direction you want to go.

What if your relationship creates the perfect storm required to break you open and bring out the highest and best within you in this lifetime? Your petty tyrant could be what the Dalai Lama would call your "noble friend" because they are equipped to reveal blocks, blemishes, obstacles, or imperfections, inhibiting you from experiencing your unfettered Infinite Loving Self. According to many near-death accounts, this person loved you enough to volunteer so you could grow leaps and bounds! Take a moment to grasp this perspective to help you pace yourself.

If you are in a petty tyrant situation where you are unable to leave, I first suggest you take a very deep breath, bring awareness to your feet, and get very anchored in your body, especially in your lower abdomen, the seat of power in your body. Consider that this person may have been divinely placed in your path to give you the irritating grain of sand that will heighten your consciousness so you can access that gorgeous pearl of great price, heightened consciousness, if you choose to accept the challenge. I know you have a long, arduous process ahead of you, but you don't have to go it alone. You are here to access the great strength from your Infinite Self while you are still in a physical body, and this is learning you can take with you when you leave this life. I hope the curriculum of this book will give you a positive framework for managing your challenge and eventually overcoming it.

One day all of my various spiritual studies merged into one line of study, I realized how good it felt to finally realize I was embarking on an established spiritual curriculum with a goal in mind. As I was musing on the good feeling of knowing that spirituality is not just a set of random different experiences, a prominent memory that was instructive for me at the time came to mind. It was on the first of September after completing my master's degree in the spring. I was feeling lost, and I was not sure that I had pursued the correct degrees for myself. I was growing into my first professional position but questioning everything about my life. I sought relief and was considering a way out of my current position. It was fall, and I had a sense it was time to return to school. It was time for my curriculum to tell me what direction to go. I was crestfallen to realize there was no curriculum for me to follow anymore; I had to forge my own life, even though I seemed so ill-equipped with answers. How would I know I was going in the right direction without a curriculum?

After deep spiritual study over many years, studying everything from near-death occurrences, brainwave consciousness, subtle energy medicine, meditation science, etc. (I could go on and on), I do believe there is a spiritual curriculum for those of us who have reached certain understandings. And just like any other advanced degree, there are perks to acquiring advanced spiritual knowledge. The advantage is that when we know how to manage our spirit's subtle energies skillfully, there is no limit to the level of joy we can feel! And from that joyful state, more opportunities abound in all directions. So, I continue cleansing my field daily as I strive to be a better conduit to commune with Infinite Love. I try not to muck up my field with emotions generated by facing daily challenges; so each year, I feel more free and fabulous. At least, that is the curriculum I am on from my level of understanding; you may have another goal in mind.

What I am trying to convey is that by learning the skills in this book, you don't have to feel powerless and demoralized in your situation. There is a curriculum to help you find your way out. From now on, you can gauge your progress in this curriculum by applying what you have learned and mastering it well. If you choose to complete the coursework, you are on the fast path to spiritual enlightenment.

I believe that Source Energy presented me with similar challenges to help you. Because I have felt energy all my life, I have always been clear that we are not here to feel like "kicked puppies," I know you don't need to waste months or years of your life feeling like a hurt animal while going through this lengthy process, either. It is simply not the truth of who we are. When we identify with our eternal spiritual self, it becomes crystal clear that demoralized energy is not part of our infinite nature!

Unfortunately, many people find themselves in difficult life circumstances where they feel defeated by the hand of cards they were dealt in this life. But powerlessness is not where our story ends; Instead, it is the precise doorway to proper calibration with the Divine that enables us to live both detached and empowered! This person in your life is here to push you to access a skillset that currently feels unnatural to you. Your discomfort is a critical tool required to undergo the necessary pruning process to access heightened consciousness. It will make you more awake at the wheel so you become aware that you're connected to a power and a force greater than yourself. The sooner you accept that your small self is officially fired, the quicker you can "trade up" with greater ease.

During the mind-body exploration for this chapter, we will continue rising up our tai chi pole. We will allow the energy of our hearts to overflow and invite the energetic current to drift up into the center of our heads. Our goal will be to have our awareness reside in our mid-brain or third eye, the place of clarity in the body. We will practice aligning to our vertical current of white light as we choose not to overlay our story. Our goal is to become receptive to pure sight. We will accomplish this by maintaining our locus of awareness within our head and not projecting it onto the situation. This is definitely more advanced work, and it will take some practice to get the hang of it. You will start to become aware that so much is happening within your energy field; navigating it all can be difficult. When we have found the seat of clarity approximately around the pineal gland, we will ask some questions: *What are you not allowing yourself to see about this person? What do you need to let yourself know about the situation? What have you not heard that this person is telling you? How is your ego's storytelling making things worse? What are you refusing to accept?* We will explore these questions and more as we continue calibrating.

Remember in the first chapter where we practiced how

to "think" of our petty tyrant from the tan tien? We will take the same approach; only this time will we "think" of our tyrant friend in the center of our head as we receive the overflowing heart and tan tien energy. We will sit there and wait for the topic to unfold. Don't expect wisdom to come down from the heavens and knock you over; however, do notice if you find yourself meandering into thinking about odd things you have never thought of in the past. Also, if you notice symbols or images emerging, acknowledge those. They often carry arcane wisdom and are loaded with meaning. Similarly, if you hear a repetitive phrase in your mind, review it for nuanced meaning. However, it is important to remember that none of this happens if you keep mentally chatting to yourself about receiving something. We must become more "empty." for greater wisdom to emerge.

You may notice it feels better to think of the situation from "within you" rather than projecting onto the problem outside of you. It just feels more comfortable and less threatening to stop projecting. Inner space is deep, isn't it? And, we have only just begun! I will be doing more public training in future years to help people further develop, as I am finally ready to share what has been unfolding within me for decades. Until now, I have primarily focused on promoting our research, not my internal work. Quite frankly, I preferred talking about the research because it was more socially acceptable. As out of the box that our research is, it was still less esoteric than this work! However, after decades of cultivation, I am ready to go public with the spiritual experiences supporting the research I championed. I will discuss this more in the later chapters.

As you practice the mind-body exploration for this chapter, start appreciating how it feels to keep your energy aligned in your soul pole. When your spirit wants to wander, tether it back to your vertical power current. We will anchor our awareness down into our tan tien, and as the energy overflows, it will rise to our neutral heart, and then let the energy float upward. Then, we will hold our awareness in our forehead to determine what we need to "see" about this situation. We will allow ourselves to **know what we know, feel what we feel, and see what we see.** We will no longer project our small story onto our greater story. We will learn to be teachable as we align with our power and allow our higher selves' wisdom to emerge. This clarity will often come with insight and illuminate "true direction."

You can find the mind-body exploration audio,
Seeing Clearly at
NuminousOnline.org/pearl
Enter the password: pearl

4

—————

INTEGRITY, DIGNITY & WORTH

Do you feel guilt regarding your relationship
with your petty tyrant?
Do you know where your worth comes from?
Are you impeccable with your integrity?
Do you stand in your dignity?

So, if you have read this far and performed the accompanying mind-body explorations, I am impressed! You have the discipline to benefit from these teachings! I didn't promise you miracles from this work. I promised you some skilled work changing your energy field so you could change some of your results. I also shared difficult information you may not have wanted to hear, espoused powerlessness, humility, and emptying yourself, and even suggested ridding yourself of self-importance. Surprisingly, you are still reading? Well done! I reiterate what I wrote at the beginning of this book: you truly have the grit required to complete the petty tyrant curriculum and significantly reduce your suffering in this life. Plus, according to near-death reports, you even get to take your advancements on the road with you when you leave this life as well!

The good news is that because you were willing to undergo all of that pruning, you can now benefit from the fruits of your new growth! However, as with all grace, it still comes with a price. There is no cheap grace. If there were, I would have found it already! However, based on your efforts thus far, mainly if you have performed the mind-body explorations, you have demonstrated you have what it takes to escort yourself into the higher realms of what this life offers. I feel incredibly privileged to be with you on this portion of your journey. Many people would have closed this book a while ago, so I am grateful for the company.

As you can see from my teaching style, I work at an organic level. I have no desire to teach cookie-cutter techniques or be the "sage from the stage." How can I take that stance when I see that most of us are already squelching custom-made wisdom desperately trying to come through us? However, I will admit I have a rare and advanced skill set of teaching people how to discipline their consciousness to access this inner wisdom and eventually reach heightened states of consciousness, so there is still plenty more for me to share. My approach has always been to lead people within their own energy while giving them the skills to cleanse and navigate it. My additional teaching goals are for you to learn how to reduce your suffering while experiencing a lot more fun so you can smile and laugh more easily. Why would we want to settle for anything less? If we must live this challenging life, let's find ways to enjoy it along the way!

Now that we have become better calibrated to both ourselves and the Divine by cultivating humility and emptying ourselves of our stories, we finally get to the "goodies!" However, caveat: if you have yet to perform each of the mind-body explorations at least five times, you are not poised well to gain the maximum benefit of what I am about to present. I reiterate that success in this work requires significantly altering your energetic landscape, often requiring careful attention and repetition. *This work is not a cognitive journey; it is an energetic one.* If you are not learning to recalibrate yourself with the Divine energetically, you won't "pick up what I am putting down." The mind-body skills are designed to help you find the space to feel at ease with yourself as you confront challenges.

Obviously, you could find these spaces inside yourself without this book, but if you are anything like me, you would fumble around a long time before that happens. I have significantly reduced your learning curve by helping you find the energetic space you seek before you experience it in the outer world. My attitude is always, "Why wait?" Delayed gratification works against us in this situation.

A well-known concept in Buddhism is that "fruit is the path." Essentially, the mind-body explorations apply this concept by helping us feel the "fruit" of our goal in our bodies first, for instance, the topics for this chapter, dignity, worth, and honor, to help us make choices that will lead us down the path to experiencing the same feelings while interacting with others. If you don't know where you are going, how will you know when you get there? We are using the mind-body explorations to "feel" into the end result of what you know is right for you.

Disciplining your nervous system to redirect your energy

field is a topic rarely, if ever, discussed, which has been my frustration over the years. As an energy sensitive, it is hard for me to live in this world and not mention my energy field. Sometimes, I marvel at my friends who have heard me discuss my energy for decades. Because they are my friends and not clients, I recently asked myself, "*Do they comprehend my comments, or are they just being polite*?" Even if they don't understand what I am saying, they have been kind enough to listen to me refer to energy for years. Those are true friends! However, when people work with me over time deep in their nervous system, they can 'talk energy" with me. They realize they have the power to change their energy fields. We share notes! Our conversations become rich with informational exchanges. I have learned so much from my "students." I put that in quotes because they are my teachers. Interacting with others has often shaped my ability to communicate inner-space topics effectively.

I value the ability to raise people's awareness to access power that is closer to them than their breath. I wish everyone knew about this approach to life. Many people are unwilling to surrender their egos to perform this deep work. We are such an "Uber eats" culture, and the old-fashioned approach to mastery is not respected as it once was. Most people want a quick answer in ten easy steps, yet, as a culture, we suffer greatly from only skimming the surface of our minds. The quality of our energy fields literally influences our entire lives, especially our mood. When people reject going inward, they leave a lot of money on the table regarding resources that can help them.

The final two chapters of this book will explore how your energy field can be calibrated to connect to Infinite Love to move into more sublime states. This book can't achieve that for you, but it can reveal the process of using challenges to up-level. Eventually, after significantly cleansing your energy field, you will apply the skills to access the pearl of heightened consciousness within you. This pearl of heightened consciousness doesn't come cheap, but it is there for the plucking if we know how to transform our suffering into joy, so let's move on to start mining our spirits for the benefits of this work.

We begin this part of our journey with unloading ourselves of guilt. Doesn't that sound fun? LOL! Deserved guilt, undeserved guilt, existential guilt, parenting guilt, food guilt, exercise guilt, and relationship guilt. Shall I go on? Review your life for a moment and look for all the pockets of guilt you briefly experience even during one day. What do you feel guilty about? What thoughts and images come to mind when you think about guilt? Do you feel guilty about what you ate for breakfast this morning? Maybe you feel guilty about how you authentically feel about something. An important question is, "Do you feel guilty about any aspect of your petty tyrant relationship?" Please take a moment and, with stark honesty, review the different areas of your life and the guilt accompanying them. Review your interactions with your family, friends, colleagues, yourself, and your petty tyrant. Are you surprised about how many pangs of guilt you feel? Which ones are the strongest?

We must come to a level of sharp awareness about how guilt has us metaphorically by our neck's short hairs in many aspects of our lives because guilt weakens us significantly. Guilt breaches our integrity, demolishes our dignity, and discourages us from accepting the highest and best. We know this deep down, but most of us never allow ourselves to stop and acknowledge the often destructive role guilt maintains in our lives. Ironically, the emotionally challenged tyrants many of us have been sparring with know our guilt spirals better than we do.

As I discussed in chapter three, sociopaths study behaviors of the emotionally healthier population because they know they are different than us. As they study us, they can become aware of the endless guilt spirals in which so many of us are deeply embroiled. We may not even be aware of how guilt pulls our strings, but petty tyrants have a sixth sense for ferreting out guilt trips invisible to us but evident to them. Once they find the scent of our guilt, they often use it to their advantage. Remember, the goal of the petty tyrant is to reveal weaknesses within us, and guilt is always our Achilles heel.

One of the mind-body exploration goals for this chapter is to make you immune to unhealthy guilt. We will purify your guilt and put it into its proper perspective. Ok, so you may be saying to yourself, "*Well, Bethany, that is impossible. I could never get rid of guilt because I did this bad thing and that bad thing, etc.*" I agree that some of your behaviors were less than stellar (Welcome to the human race. You are not unique). You may have squandered resources. You may have said things you regret. In this temporal world, you may have hurt others or yourself and are holding yourself accountable. I am grateful that you are holding yourself accountable. It means you are part of the 96% of the population with a conscience, so you make this world a better place! However, is that guilt serving you? Is your ruminating spiral of self-flagellation that you undergo over and over again serving you and the people around you now? Are you so sure you were in the "wrong" that it is causing you to be completely unteachable now? We will take guilt up to such a level that you will probably never review guilt with such excessive "know-it-all" energy ever again.

A line in *A Course In Miracles* immediately landed with me: "*Guilt's only purpose is to disrupt communication with God.*" When I read that line, I immediately stopped reading and put the book down just to think about that one line. It was like I was hit with light because I sincerely felt that statement's energetic truth. I could feel that when I was the judge and juror of my behavior, my energy stopped moving. When judging myself, I could not receive input from Infinite Love. When I was so sure I was "wrong," I was no longer teachable. The *Course* continues to explain that we never feel guilty if we bring Source Energy into every thought.

People often feel subconsciously that God/Infinite love won't want anything to do with them until they "get their act together" because they feel guilty for their behaviors. Nothing could be further from the truth. We can't be healed unless we open the dark corners of our consciousness to Divine Light. I encourage people to bring Loving Light into any of their "guilty pleasures," including smoking cigarettes and overeating, to break the hold of our ego's judgment on it.

I remember walking on the sidewalk in my early twenties, not doing anything wrong in my personal life or on the street. A police car drove by, and I felt guilty. I thought to myself, "*I am not doing anything wrong. I am not even driving! Why did I feel so guilty when a police car drove by? It doesn't make any sense!*" When I read the line from A Course In Miracles, *Guilt's only purpose is to disrupt communication with God,* I finally realized why I felt so guilty when the police car drove on the road near me that day. I had been estranged from Source Energy for many years and was not co-creating with him/her/it. I was living entirely from my little self, trying to keep myself safe with my myopic understandings of this world, and by the way, I was miserable for it!

According to The *Course*, we incarnated to co-create with the Divine, not live by our temporal ego's cravings, desires, and addictions. When we do not integrate Infinite Love into our decisions, we feel existential guilt because we are not living as we were designed to live, as co-creators. The *Course* refers to this larger part of ourselves as the "Holy Spirit," which has a slightly different connotation than many of us learned in Sunday school. In this context, the Holy Spirit is the part of our nature that remembers we are still one with Source Energy, even though we feel separate.

The truth is, we always stayed in the presence of Source. We just think we abandoned/or were abandoned by Infinite Love because we adopted a nervous system that eclipses 99.00001 percent of all the reality around us. Let me give you an actual concrete example. Human hearing can only hear from 20-20,000 Hz, but dogs can listen from 67-45,000 Hz. If you could hear like dogs, it would be like having a super-power! There is massive amounts of energetic information circling us. Ironically, we sit in the middle of this sea of infor-mation, completely oblivious and often bored because our nervous system does not register it.

Because our primitive nervous system literally can't transduce the full realm of reality around us, including the Infinite Loving energy nourishing us into being at every moment, we think we are living far away from Source. We feel distant from Infinite Love, and yet Love is closer to us than our breath! The more we discipline our nervous system, especially to feel the love nourishing us, the more we get to live in what I sometimes jokingly refer to as "yummy" places. It feels decadent. Delicious. Intoxicating. I have been surrendering my body to Source Energy (what some may call Kundalini, others may say Chi, others may say the Holy Spirit) for over thirty years, and every day, I cleanse a little more. The result is that I now get to live in beauty often.

Life still sends me curve balls because I seem to be here for full cleanup in this lifetime. However, my energy skills enable me to wear this world lightly. When I am challenged, I do what firefighters do. I "stop, drop, and roll!" What I mean by that is that I stop and notice where the challenge intrudes on my energy field, then drop my awareness into my field. I thoroughly explore the situation's emotions and issues and work through the energy kinks. I feel the swirling energies but strive to keep from attaching to them. Only after I have processed things entirely do I come to acceptance; I then roll and keep going.

It is clear to me as I am processing that whatever is challenging me is not the truth of who I am, so I only find rest with a subject if it has been distilled and cleansed. As I confront challenges, it is like I hear the beautiful music of a siren call, beckoning me to find my way back to beauty. Because I know the trigger is temporary and I will land in more extraordinary beauty after it is processed, it has become harder to be polite with well-meaning new-agers who encourage me to reach for premature resolutions or tell me to rephrase my language descriptors, thinking they are doing me a favor. I have never had the propensity to waste energy on pretense. My life would have been much easier if I could! I only say this to be accurate because I don't want to make it sound like I walk on clouds because that is not my goal. My goal is to be 100% authentic in each moment because, at these levels, truth reigns supreme. I can't hide from my energy field. I know myself too well. I have been told I can be read like a book because I find it so difficult to hold back emotion any more. The comment was made to to point out my weakness, but on another level I felt a deep satisfaction because it feels to good to be authentic.

I am pretty average, but because I am so mentally disciplined with my energy, I have lots of it to finance higher well-being. After cleaning my field for years and staring down hundreds of emotional issues, I often rest in consciousness, sometimes called the ground of being.

Being disciplined with our energy is the real theme of this book. I am teaching this skill in the context of a common gritty life issue –complex relationships— because daily conflicts reveal our energetic commerce. However, it is the same process for whatever challenges you face.

Challenges can serve as the grit in our oysters to create a valuable pearl; Suffering serves a function. Awakening quickens through wise purification of suffering. Instead of blindly reacting to adversity by ignoring it, blaming someone else for it, or loosing ourselves in substances, we apprehend it directly and more quickly to find its healthy resolution within ourselves. Through this process, we get out of the wordy stories and into the subtle energies that open an entirely new range of opportunities to confront life's challenges.

As we learn to be more discerning, we realize that we want to be more stingy in putting our energy into service to the world around us. At the end of life, it becomes evident to most people that energy is more valuable than money. Classic Shamans and healers have been aware of the preciousness of their energetic commerce since the beginning of time, but Western culture often shuts down these disciplines. We tend to worship the mind and technology while snuffing out the power of our hearts and energy. Shamans would never do that. Shamans stalk their energetic power, similar to how we stalk reviews for a new car we want to purchase. They want to account for their energy fully so they don't squander it in wasteful endeavors. A Shaman would see a fruitless repetitive guilt loop as a waste of energy and seek to resolve it as soon as possible.

Guilt is pernicious because we tend to allow it to influence us without realizing it severely inhibits us. People often lose decades of their lives to substance abuse because they have unprocessed guilt, yet love surrounds them the entire time. We can do nothing to stop this love from being directed toward us, not even obliterate ourselves with substances.

When I raised my children, I encouraged them to express all their thoughts to Source. I encouraged them that nothing is off limits, no matter how "bad" they thought they were. I told them to strive to think as if their thoughts were "written in the sky because they are." As we integrate high-frequency Infinite Love into all of our lives (not the artificial Hallmark card kind), we can't help but make different choices. Soon, our lives renovate effortlessly. We release things to make room for our new best friend, Infinite Love.

This willingness to resign from managing the universe and ourselves releases us from guilt and simultaneously enlarges us. As I often say, "When we finally take our grubby hands off the wheel," we can finally journey productively with the Divine. Until then, we are merely moving the same sand around in our sandbox. No real change occurs, and nothing new is built.

Another way to describe this process is releasing attachments. Buddhism states that all of our suffering comes from attached desires. The Sanskrit word for attachment, upādāna, means grasping or clinging. It refers to the human tendency to cling to people, things, or ideas (including guilt) in the mistaken belief that they will bring us lasting happiness and fulfillment. Attachments arise from our desire to feel secure, comfortable, and in control of our lives.

When I mention releasing attachments, maybe you asked the same questions I asked when I first heard of such a concept years ago. *"What do you mean release our attachment? Why would I bother? Where is the fun if we don't work attached to the outcome? How stupid is that? Would you tell a CEO responsible for payroll on Friday to work without attachments?? Absolutely not. That would be ridiculous!"* If you raise similar tough, cogent questions about releasing attachments, you can hear, I get it! I would often be the one asking precocious questions in spiritual circles as a young child in Christian elementary school. My hard-hitting questions about spiritual paradoxes were rarely well-received!

More than once, the teacher thought I was asking questions to be difficult and get attention. I was never trying to be difficult; I was in pursuit of truth and willing to ask for it. My skepticism continued into my adult years in spiritual circles. I had to ask the hard questions when no one else would. My gut just could never grok regurgitated Christian or new age pablum. I can be such a skeptic of spirituality myself that I even put the "law of attraction" to the test by performing research studies at city levels to see if intentions for peace had real-world impact. (I am pleased to report that our research suggests it does! We have had four successful research studies that measured reductions in violence in three US cities.) My life would have been a lot easier if I had just trusted the transcendental meditation research, but my skeptical mind could not settle for that. I am sharing my gruff interior orientation, because I want you to know I have probably asked many of the same questions you are asking about this work.

I know it may take a while for you to have enough experience with this work to confirm it for yourself, but I wanted you to rest assured that until you acquire your own results, you can borrow my faith in this process. I have asked the hardest questions for years, and I have still never abandoned this work. I don't let up, because I find that there is something undeniably integrous regarding this work, as I witness my consciousness improving year after year. No matter what spiritual work I study, I always return to these skills. I evaluate every spiritual topic by two criterion 1) Does it expand my energy field? and 2) Does it lighten my heart? After all my years of study, in my mind spirituality comes down to those two things, because they both bring me closer to Infinite Divine Love. Spirituality is *that* simple! I like simple! If you like this approach, you may want to gain access to my **Concsiousness Athlete** bank of meditations, as they are all designed with those two goals in mind, because I apply these skills daily.

Releasing attachments can sound elusive and not fun; I want you to know I understand. I share your hard questions, and after years of qualifying this topic, I am here to tell you that Buddha really was on to something! Releasing attachments, rocks! LOL! Jesus also demonstrated this concept when he was hungry after being in the wilderness for 40 days and tempted with food, wealth, and power. Jesus denied those things because he knew his relationship with the Divine would sustain his future *epic* challenge (understatement!) more than earthly attachments. When you pull your spirit back from things you are attached to, you now have the space in your consciousness to feel fabulous! Ask those hard questions, then move into your energy field and align it with your soul pole to access answers. Just to clarify, in my opinion, there is absolutely no problem with acquiring wealth or possessions; it is just to the extent that people distort their energy field to obtain them that is destructive, which is why there are so many addicted wealthy people.

Continue exploring this work's alchemy by releasing your guilt attachments and aligning your energy field with great love, integrity, dignity, and worth. As you navigate your difficult situation, your life will start shifting within a few months. Don't be afraid to set intentions for resolution, although they often come in far different forms than expected. Also, be aware that your answers may come with shifts to your energy field.

Suddenly, you realize you are responding differently, and you have no idea why! For instance, I remember being a carbohydrate addicted young woman. I was asked to go to a bakery to pick up a cake for the office. While there, I saw the pastries in the glass display and thought, "*As long as I am here, I may as well treat myself to a pastry.*" Then this foreign thought occurred, I said to myself, "*Nah, I don't feel like having one right now.*" I immediately looked left and right and laughed and jokingly said to myself, "*Who said that?*" I could tell something so fundamental in my personality had shifted due to my energy work. My energy had changed. It no longer unconsciously hemorrhaged to carbohydrates! That was a fun day that demonstrated my energetic efforts with a tangible real life result!

Words rarely worked for me. Often, you can tell me

through words what I need to do, but these words don't land. I need energetic answers. Even as a child, words did not help me much, because my energy field would not let me be satisfied with surface answers. I knew my spirit was bigger than my body, and confining my opinions to the body didn't work for me either. Often, words seemed so shallow and incomplete that they did not heal me. But, when I checked in with my spirit, which was much larger in my perception, I could feel that there was always a direction to go, and it was always toward more wholeness. The direction was beyond a description in words but was always toward greater energetic integrity. I finally realized the correct answer would always be where my energy felt healthy, balanced, and whole. The correct answer was where my energy field did not collapse or cower. The correct answer was where I could stand tall in my worth. My eternal self refused to let me surrender to reconciling spending the rest of my life as a hurt puppy.

At this point in my development, I know we all have eternal selves who would never want us to settle for anything less. By dedicating yourself to calibrating your field to the Divine through these mind-body explorations, you will find a space of greater integrity within you. Again, this work is costly. The paywall to this wisdom is training in the discipline of calibrating your energy field. The good news is that the internal effects are immediate, which encourages us to continue cultivating the inward discipline before our outer lives change.

Every day, I calibrate my small self to my soul pole and clean my energy field by returning to the well of Infinite Love, and every day, I live more and more from the loving sweetness of my Infinite Self. Conversely, this also means that every day, I must sacrifice something from my small self to make room for my "big" self. Any attachments of guilt, sorrow, and loss must go. Some days, I explore emotions more before letting them go, but I always know the punch line is...Let...Them....Go.... Full stop!

I am so clear that clinging to attachments only contributes to my suffering that I am known in my circles for this phrase, *"Become intolerant of feeling miserable."* I encourage this for people because I know misery is not the truth of who I am and is not the truth of who you are, either. I am an eternal being of love connected to the infinite cosmos, and so are you! Misery is a stagnant, slow, sticky, dirty, collapsing energy that sticks to the ego. We feel liberated and free when our energy fields are clean and flowing. So, I refuse to settle for swimming in misery when I know I have the skills to clean and purify my energy to get back to my buoyant eternal self.

When you start to understand your energetic commerce with the world, you know that misery is an option caused by attachments. This means that a portion of our spirit leaves our body and attaches to places, people, things, and (drumroll please) guilt! When too much of our spirit is out of our body financing attachments, we create a credit balance, generating depression and physical illness. When we feel guilt, we sabotage by limiting ourselves to the good things in life. Our tangled energy is not available to finance the more expensive and positive emotions such as love, joy, and sweetness. When we pull our spirit back from attachments and reinsert that energy deep into ourselves, we have more energy to finance our happiness.

Buddhist leaders love to discuss how attachments lead to suffering but rarely discuss the surprising reciprocal results; *releasing attachments leads to joy!* People would be more willing to let go of their attachments if they could feel the genuine relief of release ahead of time. If you have an authentic experience of releasing attachments, you don't have to take my word for this! You won't even want to take on attachments again. They will feel too confining, and you understand why Buddha and Jesus discouraged them at every turn.

We will begin our last meditation by imagining throwing anything we feel guilty about into a Divine Fire. Remember, when we feel guilty, it is because our small self wants to be the judge and juror so we can run the show. We are generally control freaks trying to be managers of the universe. We want to have all the answers and be in charge, which makes us miserable because we know we are inherently incomplete. However, as we learn to review all our thoughts to be cleansed and purified by Infinite Love, we receive the healing benefits of living close to love. Love shows us how to reconcile our guilt. It may instruct us on how to perform external actions to reconcile the wrongs we feel guilty about or it may instruct us that we merely need to forgive ourselves for such behavior so the guilt can exit our system for good.

Remember, one of the roles of the Petty Tyrant in our lives is to provide a mirror of where our weaknesses lie, which will virtually always be associated with our guilt. When we feel trapped in a relationship with someone who we believe has power over us, we are often forced to scrutinize ourselves under intense pressure. By cleansing ourselves of the guilt weakening us, we move into a healthy state of detachment, finally leaving space for the Divine wisdom to emerge. This emerging connection to the Divine reveals our latent power.

I want you to have fun with this mind-body exploration

as you release the guilt restrictions holding you back. Smile as you do this! You may even want to take your hand to the area in your body tightening with guilt and imagine grabbing the block and tossing it toward the Divine flame with flair. Go ahead; it is not the real you, but it is blocking you from the Infinite Love that *is* the real you. So have fun flinging it away from yourself to be purified in the crucible of Infinite Love. Soon, you will feel lighter and happier, and a strangely familiar, loving presence will emerge. This is your I Am self, the real authentic you.

I can hear many of you say now, "*What??? Let go of my guilt? Won't that make me even more of a horrible person? Isn't that what you said sociopaths are like? Who will I be without it if I let go of my guilt?*" Like all spiritual truths, this is another great paradox. The sooner we release thinking that we know it all, including assuming that we are to be judged for our guilt, the sooner a wise, Intelligent Love can reveal a higher wisdom than our own. This intelligence loves everyone (including your petty tyrant) more than you do, is more objective than you(or your petty tyrant), and cares for everyone (including your petty tyrant) more than you do. But if we keep ourselves bound to our egotistical understandings, we will never feel Infinite Love's expansiveness, so we will never feel the expansiveness of heightened consciousness.

As we create space for Infinite Love in our lives, we become delightfully free from some negative consequences of our creations that enslaved us to unhealthy guilt. In this meditation, we will throw our burdens into a Divine fire. By submitting them to the cleansing flame, our subconscious will work to help us release toxic attachments so we can live with greater freedom, clarity, and purpose. But don't take my words for the truth of any of this. Try it yourself. After earnestly performing this meditation once, you will discover you have the key to release yourself from your guilt spiral that you may have not even realized was strangling you.

Another quote from the *Course* illuminates this process more, "*The giving up of judgment, the obvious prerequisite for hearing God's Voice, is usually a fairly slow process, not because it is difficult, but because it is apt to be perceived as personally insulting.*" What if we did not expect ourselves to know all the answers? What if we were on a "need to know basis" with the Divine and we were ok with that? Do children insist on knowing everything about their futures? And yet, they have more playful hearts. Maybe the *Course* suggests that if we let go of our judgments, we are more likely to emulate the light-hearted consciousness of children and enter that mysterious "Kingdom within" that Jesus often mentioned.

Who will you be without being bound by existential guilt? You will be more kind, wise, tolerant, joyful, and free because you will have surrendered to the alchemical process of being purified by love. You become so pleased when you realize you don't have to be king or queen of the universe. Whew! What a relief! We don't have to know it all, be it all, or have it all! We can rest in ourselves, honor our humanity, including our mistakes, and allow them to be healed by greater wisdom. It is a bargain if we can get the hang of being both humble and great!

After releasing guilt in the mind-body exploration, we will practice cleansing the rest of our soul pole. This means moving through the crown of our head and moving our awareness about 1.5 to 3 feet above the head to feel what is often called the ninth chakra. As we progress from the earth to above our heads, we will cleanse the pole with a scintillating iridescent pearly white light. We will access this by projecting our locus of awareness through the crown chakra and "poke around" with our awareness until we find an area that feels like a doorway. We will "open" this door way and allow golden pearlescent light to download into us.

I have done this work with people on the massage table in my office for years. More than once, people would ask me, "*Are you anointing me with oil?*" or "*Did you poor oil over my head?*" I had no oil. I was opening this portal to the Divine for them, which is a doorway of sorts to Infinite Love. In the mind-body exploration, you may experience such a phenomenon. I believe that this is the process that David was experiencing when he wrote in Psalm 23, "*You anoint my head with oil. My cup runs over. Surely goodness and mercy shall follow me all the days of my life; And I will dwell in the house of the Lord, forever.*" It is remarkable when we correlate spiritual texts with neuroscience and subtle energy phenomenon. Suddenly, phrases that we know and love become multi dimensional, and we realize that we have only scratched the surface of such profound truths.

If you feel subtle energies cascading over your head, possibly feeling like oil moving downward, don't discount it. It is real, which is why David was saying, "*I will dwell in the house of the Lord forever,*" because he could feel the surety of God's presence. The more we do this work, the more we realize if we calibrate ourselves, we could live in "goodness and mercy" permanently if we trained our nervous system properly (my first book delves into this topic). We realize that our locus of awareness can discover all sorts of energetic nuances around us if we know how to direct it skillfully. It took me a long time to honor these experiences since they did not come with written instructions. However, I have learned that they introduce a wisdom that may not be instructive verbally but nonverbally point the way to better frolicking with the Divine!

Traditional Taoist teachings say that our taiji pole or soul is where we individuate as human beings. Eastern medicine espouses that the white light in our soul pole provides the energetic nourishment required to hold our soul in our bodies. I like to think of our soul pole as similar to taking a palmful of water from the ocean. The water in our palm is still part of the ocean but it is its own distinct entity. Our soul pole is where we become a portion of the sea of Infinite Love. Whether or not this vertical power current is truly our "soul" is irrelevant to me. Regardless of what books or people say, my measuring stick for any spiritual modality is if my field feels more integral and whole.

Working with this power highway of the energy field is undeniably strengthening. In this meditation, we will allow our locus of awareness to drift above our heads and set an intention to receive a download from Infinite Love as we feel the integrity of its light coming down through us and into the earth below us. We will practice maintaining our integrity line as we imagine facing our stressors. When we notice circumstances that snag our energy, we pull our energy back into our soul pole.

Next, we will take this work to an even more advanced level. We will practice holding our soul's integrity through our fortified soul pole while mentally rehearsing being in the presence of our petty tyrant. Our field will want to cave; we will want to betray ourselves by letting our field collapse and dissolving our soul pole. Instead, we will resist those impulses and practice maintaining our soul's integrity in the presence of our tyrant teacher. We will keep our shoulders back and our heads up, looking eye to eye with our tyrant as we observe how our energy field distorts. We will remember that they offer us an opportunity to reestablish our soul's integrity.

I will let you in on a secret. I will tell you this now, but you will more fully comprehend what I am sharing after practicing the mind-body exploration for this chapter about three to five times. This is an incredibly advanced practice, but most people are too attached to their resentments to consider it. Ideally, it is best to see your petty tyrant as an equal participant in your learning if you can. You are their mirror, and they are yours. No one wants to do this. We inherently resist it. But, if you see your tyrant with gratitude for revealing aspects of yourself that needed healing, surprisingly, you will feel greater respect and dignity for yourself. This occurs, because you are reaching the oneness state, which I will discuss more fully in future books.

Eventually, if you are like so many others I have taught, you will be surprised by a wave of self-love and respect that surges through your body, sometimes with a smile. We realize that until we can hold our dignity in the face of injustices, we can't experience the best of our energies. If we look down on anyone, we look down on ourselves. As the work of Paul Selig states repeatedly, "*What you damn, damns you back!*" Nowhere is this clearer than when we are working in our energy field. This person has given you the gift of revealing places where you do not own your worth. You may even be surprised that when you tap into your Divine dignity, you may want to spontaneously transfer that honor to your tyrant friend. You will also notice you can only stand in your full dignity if you honor theirs. But don't push yourself too much. Just remain where you can feel healed and whole, the rest will come over time.

As we start allowing Infinite love to help us make all of our decisions, we become happier. High-frequency love often feels less like an emotion but a strength. This love has no dogma. However, it honors all living things, including our petty tyrant. So, we feel growing dignity within us as we gain respect for our petty tyrant and the wisdom they have unlocked within us. We realize our soul pole has greater integrity when we honor theirs. As we get familiar with humbling our ego and airing out our psyche, we realize this challenge offered us an opportunity to step out into our larger nature. We have become a genie who escaped from a bottle and don't want to go back in! The new air is too crisp, well-being flows too well, and our spirit feels too light to ever want to succumb to your old story of petty tyrant again. You now live as if all your emotions are written in the sky, so your spirit is never stifled again.

You are now living in a manner that properly calibrates you to receive your Divine inheritance. As you live from this greater integrity, you begin to feel worthiness down to your bone marrow—a worthiness that does not come from any human being or temporal position but from Source itself. You have become a citizen of the field and experience a profound clarity that you are as worthy as any dignitary.

As you grow into this new space, your commerce with the world permanently changes. You find yourselves making different decisions from a place of honor within yourself. Awareness of your inherent dignity generates a deep, abiding sense of self-worth. As we practice releasing our baggage and opening to the Loving Intelligence that connects us all, we realize as *A Course In Miracles* suggests, we don't have to be love, because we *are* love! As dense, energetic blocks release from our fields, gratitude swells to the surface spontaneously. We learn that our authentic state is a one of deep gratitude and appreciation. We start embracing life with a sweet abandon and a zest for life that reminds us of being children again.

You don't have to worry about moving into the selfish space of the sociopath because your heart becomes so large that you realize to maintain its highway to heaven, you must see everyone through the eyes of oneness. In this space, there is no "other." Your petty tyrant is your teacher and deserves respect. The Dalai Lama called the Chinese who occupied Tibet his "noble friends" and said that no one taught him to love more than the Chinese who destroyed his family and country. As Don Juan taught Carlos Castaneda, *"Self-importance can't be fought with niceties."* We needed our petty tyrants to ruthlessly clean the house of our small, petty selves so we could emerge into our loving, expansive selves. This is the point in your training that you start to see your petty tyrant as "friend and equal."

When you hold the space in this meditation of honoring your petty tyrant without cowering, you can start transferring this work to interactions with your tyrant teacher in the physical. If you can't hold your honor energetically in the etheric, you may be unable to do it physically, so use meditation to warm up to the process.

We will end the meditation, requesting peace as the final resting place of this relationship. *A Course In Miracles* reminds us that peace is all we ever want in any situation. We may wish for money, a partner, or a house, but take that further. We pray for money, a home, or a partner because we believe they will bring us peace. But what if we just skipped to the peace? What if we felt peace along the way to peace? After all, you could get the money, house and partner, and still be miserable. So, ask for the highest, peace, and while you are at it, throw in love and truth because the universe is abundant with these ideals. They never end!

As you learn how to rid yourself of guilt, strengthen your integrity, and access your inherent dignity in the etheric, eventually, your interactions with your petty tyrant in the physical will change. It may not be pretty, either. Sometimes, forests need to burn entirely before they can generate new growth. I have often said, "*Sometimes peace requires causing a ruckus on the way out.*" Many books can support you in that strategic part of your journey. I am here to give you a roadmap to your spirit and how to heal and repair it, which can help point directions to explore physical solutions. I suggest you continue performing these mind-body explorations to help you find behaviors that result in respect, integrity, dignity, and growth. As you learn to maintain the integrity of your vertical power current while simultaneously learning to be humble and teachable, these spaces often unlock mysteries for you, and new options eventually emerge.

At this point in my understanding, anchoring in our Divine worth and dignity is the real spiritual game we are playing in this lifetime. We are not here to earn a bunch of money, have a big house, and be admired by others. Those are very nice, but there are plenty of depressed, miserable rich well-known people. In my mind, our goal in the physical is to heal our souls of feeling separate from the Divine through playing the game of "Divine wake-up." To wake up in the physical body and say, "*Ohhhh...That is right! I remember!! I am an eternal being in a temporal physical body! This third dimension is just my game board. I can unplug from the dream of being a purely physical being and play the game remembering, I am eternal,"* which offers us far more options to explore!

No one helps us advance in this cosmic game more than petty tyrants. They appear to deconstruct our psyche so we can reassemble it with such tensile strength that nobody could similarly break us again. We become more beautiful human beings, similar to how the Japanese art of Kintsugi makes pottery more beautiful after it has cracked. This ancient art form includes melting gold to solder together broken pottery pieces. The pottery becomes stronger and more beautiful due to its brokenness, as streaks of gold hold the broken pieces together. Through this work, our soul becomes Kintsugi pottery -more elegant than before it was "broken."

Speaking of beauty in the context of our struggles may not sound possible. I understand. I did not always speak this way. I came from a family where addictions and depression ran rampant. It took me years to break through into these spaces, but I often felt like I had my fingers on the tale of a tiger. The more I released blocks in my field, the more I could sense the presence of something fabulous on the other side. In fact, I learned that following these good feelings will take you all the way up to heaven! (Discussed in my first book).

I suggest a way not to get discouraged. Always notice how different you feel when you begin a meditation compared to when you end the meditation. In these meditations, you will often feel a significant difference. If so, note those positive differences and bank on them! They mean that you have moved the needle a little bit; imagine if you kept at it and moved the needle even more in the same direction? Feeling even slightly better tells you that you are definitely moving in the correct direction for the full release. Stay with this unfoldment to access the gorgeousness that is your birthright.

Please have fun with this meditation. Allow yourself to "stretch into" your expansive self. Feel the joy of releasing burdens that do not belong to your Infinite soul. Imagine freeing yourself of these third-dimensional weights as you shake them free like a dog shaking off water in his coat after swimming in a lake. Practice this meditation at least five times. Learn to embrace the strength of feeling energy running unimpeded through your energy system and the joy that comes from such integrity. Practice being free, being love, and being you!

You can find the mind-body exploration audio,
Integrity, Dignity, and Worth at
NuminousOnline.org/pearl
Enter the password: pearl

5

REPLACING OUR ATTACHMENTS WITH NOURISHING LOVELIGHT

What attachments are you holding on to?
What do you hope happens regarding
your petty tyrant relationship?
Who would you be without your struggles?
What would it feel like to be at peace with
whatever is happening in your life?

In this final chapter, we will review what we have learned and then close with a final powerful skill that, when used regularly, will help you continue clearing your energy field to experience more sublime states of consciousness. As you progress through these chapters, you may not have realized that you have been learning the fine art and science of enlightened detachment. By calling your spirit back to your body and strengthening your soul pole in the presence of your petty tyrant through these mind-body explorations, you have been creating a more defined and cleaner energy field surrounding your body. See! I told you, detachment isn't so bad! Humility isn't either! It is liberating when you get used to it!

Ironically, you probably did not even realize you were cultivating detachment. However, I do hope you realize that you are feeling more "yourself" as you progress through these mind-body explorations. You are becoming calibrated to your own Spirit. You are cleansing it of temporal limiting debris generated by your relationships that are blocking you from your authentic signal. The more you clean your field, the more free you are to be yourself.

My goal is for you to connect the dots so that you can change your state of consciousness by changing your energy field. This realization may inspire you to explore subtle energies to enhance your life significantly. Maybe you learned something valuable through this process and realized the conflict with your petty tyrant inspired you to take the Heightened Consciousness Spiritual Law School curriculum and yield its benefits. This is where you approach the idea that you might even be thankful for the petty tyrant struggle that returned you to yourself. Are you there yet? Well, even if you are not, spoiler alert: if you keep up this work, you will be! Let's review our process now.

In Chapter One, we learned about gaining mastery over our locus of awareness and anchoring it to the lower tan tien as we faced our petty tyrant. We also learned how the location of our locus of awareness significantly influences the quality of our lives and how undisciplined our minds are at directing our awareness.

In chapter two, we moved up our vertical taiji pole and explored maintaining a neutral heart. We learned how to release heart walls toward our tyrant friends to mute any stories we tell ourselves about them. We learned the discipline of subjugating our egos to hear the transcendent, loving wisdom of the heart.

In chapter three, we learned hard truths about the human population and how it behooves spiritual people to release their lofty ideals approximately twelve percent of the time to account for emotionally challenged individuals who don't have regard for our humanity. We allow ourselves to "see" people as they present themselves. We are sure to refrain from letting our spiritual orientation influence us so that we don't indiscriminately project our goodwill onto those who don't have the normal emotional palette range to reciprocate. We allow ourselves to feel what we feel, know what we know, and see what we see without a guilt-trip spiritual overlay on how we are "supposed" to see people.

In chapter four, we had fun releasing pernicious guilt strings to become more clear vessels for Divine inspiration. We practiced becoming aware of where we differentiate from the sea of Infinite Love around us in our ninth chakra above the head. We invited a liquid love to pour down into our vertical energy highway to maintain our soul integrity as we mentally rehearse, holding our power in the presence of our petty tyrant. We resist the impulse to cave in on ourselves or to bend our primary power current. If we feel it is safe and ok, we honor the role of our petty tyrant in our lives, as we learn that condemning someone only contracts our field.

You might have thrown away this book if I had mentioned honoring your petty tyrant teacher in chapter one before we did our energy work together. But, if you have been doing the mind-body explorations as prescribed, you may be experiencing the wisdom of this subtle but powerful work. It feels good to be energetically congruent; ideally, we become addicted to this state of consciousness. When we live from our integrity, we experience inherent dignity and unassailable self-worth; anything short of that is not who we are.

We are infinite beings. Our bodies only exist to let people know where our Spirit is in the third dimension. The purpose of the Heightened Consciousness Spiritual Law school initiation is to pull your identity from the plug of the temporal earthly world and transfer it to our eternal nature so we obtain its benefits. Most of us would never undergo this process if everything were rainbows and unicorns in our lives. When challenges and petty tyrants appear, they give us the precise friction to propel us toward growth that we would resist without them.

We have discussed how petty tyrants reveal our attachments. They provide an opportunity to pull our spirits back from unhealthy thoughts and desires so we can reinsert this energy back into our energy field, which helps us harness our power for more exciting pursuits. As our energy floods back to us, our soul pole strengthens. We start to garner a bank of energy that helps us finance emotions of well-being, such as love, joy, and peace.

In this final chapter, now that you have pulled more of your spirit back from the 3D world, we will reconnect you to the portion of your infinite nature that always 'remembers' you have never left the side of Source Energy. You see, you are now more humbled and calibrated to remember the glory of you! We have now made space for you to reconnect to the part of you that water can't get wet, and fire can't burn. The part of you that remembers the sublime nature of your true eternal self.

In some traditions, this may be referred to as your Christ

self, Buddha nature or your I am presence. Many spiritual traditions refer to this truth through words, but words don't give us a road map because this is not a cognitive journey. It is an energetic journey. Words are far too limiting to discuss the transcendent nature of God. So, often, when people hear about such concepts, they disregard them, thinking that reaching your Christ self is unobtainable. Yet, in this truth lies the beauty of your being, because your Christ self is literally infused into your current personality. Our job is to be like Michelangelo when he sculpted David. Michelangelo did not create the statue of David, he only removed the pieces of marble that were not David. Our role in this work is to remove our energetic blocks so we can identify more with our eternal **I am** self. As Meister Eckhart insightfully noted, *"spirituality has much more to do with subtraction than it does with addition."*

It may take a while to grasp the power of this work entirely. Remember where you started and how you have already made great strides. Keep at it; you will. I was compelled to perform this work for decades, but most of that time, I did not have an apparent reason to pursue it with such fervor. I would often grumble at what appeared to be "lack of results." My friends could tell you I have bitched with the best of them!! But, as I traveled through my trials and tribulations, I saw many of my internal struggles dissolve through consistent alchemical themes shared in this book. Now, I bank on these themes because I can feel the difference in my consciousness. One day, you may wake up and feel a crisp, clean, scintillating energy surrounding you. While appreciating the accompanying well-being, you may even say to yourself, *"It was worth it!"* The best news? Is that that your newfound well-being is only the beginning, because Love is infinite. So the real question is, *just how good do you want to feel?*

We can keep "trading up" indefinitely because love has no end. In my first book, I wrote about three individuals who took this path into heightened well-being, including Brother Lawrence, a lay Carmelite monk from the sixteenth century. We know the name of this non-educated kitchen worker because dignitaries would come to sit by him to hear his wisdom. Brother Lawrence disciplined his locus of awareness to bring God/Source Energy into every activity he performed. After ten years of this practice, he reached a significant buoyant state of consciousness; after thirty years, he was so perpetually "high" that he kept his Divine happiness to himself so others would not think he was "mad." So, I will ask again, seriously: *How good do you want to feel?* The sky is not even the limit! The real question is, *How bad do you want it?*

Because I felt my energy field so strongly, I had to follow this path, because the blocks in my field felt like rocks in my shoe. You can only take a few steps with an object in your shoe before you have to stop and remove it. That has been my process. Every challenge that emerged had to be addressed not only in the external world but in my energy field so I could feel more at ease.

After teaching mind-body exploration skills for decades, I have observed how these skills can powerfully shift people's orientations in their lives. However, practicing each mind-body exploration only five times is not nearly enough. I suggested practicing them five times each as you progress in this book so you learn how the individual explorations of the overall spiritual law curriculum fit together. However, you may need to practice them dozens of time times before your energy field maintains its new direction. You may find that you are drawn to one of the meditations more than the others. Go with that! That is your spirit telling you where to work. You will know when you are done with it. To continue cleaning your energy field, you may want to consider subscribing to my bank of Consciousness Athlete explorations to deepen your skills after you reach a level of mastery in these meditations.

It is a good idea always to transfer these mind-body exploration skills into your daily activities. For instance, when walking down the hall during a busy day at work, bring your awareness to your feet so you ground your energy on the go. When you hear your child complain about school, try maintaining a neutral heart. Download liquid light from your ninth chakra when you feel intimidated by life. When acknowledging that you may not getting the complete story from your petty tyrant, ground yourself in your tan tien, release your heart, and then move your awareness behind your eyes, so you can intend to clearly "see" the situation.

My favorite way to bring these skills into daily life is through exercise. I savor being able to walk alone to bring awareness into my legs and feet. I strive to ground my energy so my whole body sinks into my ground of being as I walk. I crave this state of consciousness, similar to how people crave food. I make my exercise time a treat for myself at the end of a productive day. I have been disciplined with exercise for decades because it helps my energy field. I don't just exercise for physical results. After a long day of serving the world, I want to feel release and expansion, so I often move slowly and with intent, as I swim and walk at the end of the day. I try to exercise as the martial artists train, from a "relaxed power." I often ask myself, *"How can I exercise with only about*

70% effort so my energy field does not contract as I move?" I suggest you play with your locus of consciousness while exercising and find the most delightful places to park it. For instance, I loved playing with my locus of awareness while performing in the 105° Hot Yoga Bikram balance sequence. When my mind flickered, my body flickered. But as I practiced over time, I delighted in my ability to hold my mind and body entirely still in the challenging balance poses. A still mind is it's own unique kind of happiness.

Eventually, maintaining awareness of your locus of consciousness becomes second nature. Repetitively lightening your heart, expanding your energy field, and strengthening your soul pole yields infinite dividends over time. I refer to this lifestyle approach as becoming a *Consciousness Athlete* because we are conditioning our energy fields to maintain a happy buoyancy, similar to how athletes condition their bodies to perform well. The skills you are learning in this book are the basic building blocks, but there are many ways to enhance your field. When I worked with one group to explore and clean our energy fields together for six and a half years, all of us experienced a significant increase in mood baselines over time.

Each time you practice calibrating your field, you discipline yourself to stay in command of your Spirit, which keeps you from squandering your life force. Instead of hemorrhaging your power unconsciously through repeating negative stories, you have learned to be more discerning and to send your Spirit off on pursuits that will only lead you to greater peace. This is a process. It will take time, but now you have skills to apply to any challenge that will up-level your energy so you have more fun playing the "Divine Wake-up" game.

As I faced challenge after challenge in my external world, often the only refuge I had was to dive into my energy field for relief. Eventually, I learned to count every internal shift as a win. I recognized I was actually "doing something" even if outward results did not appear. In his book *Atomic Habits*, James Clear discusses the "remarkable results of tiny habits." He mentions how people can change their lives by only 1% each day and yield significant results. This curriculum demonstrates Clear's point extremely effectively. I have often wondered where I would be without repetitively making 1% changes over the years. Fellow Consciousness Athletes would ask the same question as well. This work is always available to us to change our lives twenty-four hours a day, seven days a week. This pearl of great price, consciousness, holds great value, and yet it costs nothing.

I am often perplexed by the infinite amount of beautiful energy surrounding us, yet most of us have no idea how to access its blessings. I wish I could share this information with people who are struggling with substance abuse. They wrestle with substances because they are desperate for relief from existential anxiety. I have encouraged you to become humble to help us access Source Energy. Similarly, it is common for people with addictions to pull external circumstances that humble them so much, they are finally willing to consider accepting help from a Loving Source to help them heal.

After writing that paragraph, I felt drawn to Google the twelve steps of Alcoholics Anonymous to review them. As I read them, I smiled at the similarities with this curriculum. I am amused to realize this book is the energetic correlate of those twelve steps! *Interesting!*

I recognize that subtle energy work is discouraged in

most rehabilitation centers, and it saddens me that people who were willing to destroy their lives to feel good are not being introduced to the very thing they were seeking through substances. For some gift of grace, I had a place to go within myself when the chips were down. I knew I could apply a healthy discipline to remove my anxiety, but others have not been blessed with such expertise or experiences. It is my life's work to help others find the treasure within them, so I have championed the Resonant Peaceful Cities Project through the nonprofit I founded, NUMINOUS. Through this work, we help people tune their nervous systems toward these heightened states.

By performing these fundamental tools, you won't have the long learning curve I did. If you repeatedly apply these skills, you will progress more rapidly because I offer you shortcuts I did not have. When you know what the universe asks of you in any situation, your confusion is cut short because you know your way back to wholeness. Like any path, the road returning to wholeness becomes more defined every time you take it. You may have to discipline your spirit dozens of times before your energy field maintains its shape. However, it is worth it to finally live in that peace. Be patient. Stay steady. Sometimes, the only documentation of your progress will be the changing quality of your energy field, which may reflect little in your external life. But you can always count your shift in mood toward well-being as your progress metric.

After teaching esoteric topics for many years, I have learned that information sometimes needs to be repeated differently to resonate. Before we proceed with learning our next set of skills, I will summarize this book's approach from a different perspective.

All of our earthly suffering is reflected in our energy fields. When we are in a negative or a positive rumination loop, a place in our energy field is breached. Healing aims to terminate this loop and eliminate the energetic imbalances so we no longer hemorrhage our power to attachments. Sometimes, people must energetically cauterize their Spirit through repetitive subtle energy skills before the hemorrhaging stops. Our nervous systems have been working without our direction for decades, and it can often take significant willpower to turn the ship around.

As I said at the beginning of this book, this information is not a "quick fix." This work is "simple, but not easy." However, you will eventually go into your energy field and notice it is cleaner. Things will have changed. You might start working on a familiar block, which suddenly collapses immediately. When this happens, *you know you did it!* You were chipping away at the block regularly, and then one day, it released along with the emotional baggage it held. That is a great feeling! The more you repair your energy field, the more you see that your hard work pays off. This progress will make you feel more at ease with yourself and your circumstances. Eventually, it will reflect in your external life. At that point, you might surprise yourself when you say regarding resolving your petty tyrant situation, "*Nice if it happens, nice if it doesn't.*" Because you cleared the mental noise around the problem, you are less attached to outcomes

In this final chapter, we continue our subtle energy-cleansing efforts by cultivating a long-term relationship with Light! I have always had an intriguing relationship with Light, and I hope you will, too, after practicing the mind-body exploration for this chapter. As a child, I had a few experiences where Jesus' energy appeared to me as just a golden Light. Light is symbolic in all religions as it relates to divine wisdom and understanding.

My first experience with potent Light occurred in my twenties, sitting in a meditation circle. The instructor invited us to imagine a pillar of Light in the center of our circle and watch how the Light beamed in all directions. As I "imagined" the Light reaching me, I was literally physically "pushed back" into my chair, very similar to a rough plane takeoff. I could feel Light's power. I could feel it's strength.

It has been common for me to wake in the middle of the night with Light streaming around me. I would brush off these experiences for years and never mention them to people. Yet, these episodes strengthened my resilience in some of my most vulnerable moments. The Light healed me, but it did not make my life any easier. Frankly, these midnight meetings with the Divine annoyed me more than anything else because it was often impossible to return to sleep, and it never seemed to offer me any tangible benefits for the disruption.

Eventually, after a *very* long time... I came to accept these experiences were significant. They were not to be brushed aside. I finally accepted that I was on a more extensive journey than I ever realized; I was in a deep, long-term, ongoing relationship with Light! I hadn't wanted to acknowledge this because I felt the Light experiences had no earthly value and did not seem to lessen my load. Eventually, I started to connect the dots. They would often appear during my most onerous times. These experiences gave me the energy downloads and resilience needed to overcome the ample resistance to my mission. Light has become my "go to" for all situations in life, and I finally feel comfortable enough to share these experiences.

One time, I was staying at an Airbnb in Pennsylvania for meditation EEG biofeedback training, where many people experienced equipment failures, delaying all of our studies. I woke in the middle of that night after my first day and decided to meditate. Suddenly, I can't even really explain it, but liquid Light started pouring down the crown of my head and into my body, making me shake with spiritual power. In front of my minds eye, I saw the the scene of earlier in the day when participants were staring down at all of their devices, frustrated with the technical difficulties they were experiencing. Tears started streaming down my face with love for all of humanity, especially those relative strangers! I witnessed through a cosmic knowing that everything that had gone "wrong" that day was, actually, divinely ordained. Everything happening was "right"; our level of consciousness was making things "wrong." I remember shaking my head thinking as I prepared to return the next day and remembering my love attack in the middle of the night, saying to myself. *"What the freak was that?"*

My most fruitful moments were often when things were the most bleak. During these times, Light would appear. I rarely, if ever, told people about these experiences because they were odd and out of the norm. However, I did feel the download of strength that accompanied them.

I may only have had the resolve to complete our peace meditation research studies because I had these spiritual reinforcement experiences at 3:00 AM. I experienced extensive pushback from most organizations and people for our "invisible" research to impact crime through intention. The general public had a hard time considering that intentions could be associated with reductions in violence, especially in the early days of our research. I now realize the light was helping me overcome this resistance. Here are some random examples of resistance I faced while I mostly financed this research as a single mom taking care of young children and elderly parents: an international local community service group mocked me after a presentation. I had to attend a hearing with the teachers' union after proposing teaching mindfulness in schools before it was widely accepted. I was snubbed by a Christian medical practice in our focus area with a prayer room, and yet we were doing essentially prayer research. I remember being on a date and my companion teasing me by reminding me that I thought I could influence crime with my mind. I laughed with him because I had to admit it sounded funny. Many assumed I could face all these challenges because I had a "corporate husband" supporting me, yet nothing was further from the truth. I often said, I have been rejected so many different types of people, but I was relentless in my mission. My resolve to champion our research made no sense. I can only attribute that resilience to downloads of potent Light in the middle of the night because I would wake in the morning, ready to tackle this mysterious process all over again. Now, that we have our successful data, I feel more comfortable about it all, but for most of those years, I lived in the unknown everyday.

Throughout the years, often when I was sick, I started referring to my burgeoning energetic discipline with Light as "God Bathing." This is when I would meditate lying on my bed and imagine a light cleansing my energy field, similar to how light changes the blood flow in our bodies as we tan in the sun. If there was a place in my body that was hurting, I would imagine a warm light inviting the blocks in my energy field to clear so healing blood flow would move throughout the area, cleaning the dense energy.

I remember one evening, I was sick with Covid, and my lungs felt like they were hardening. I was starting to feel as if there was an iron lung around me without the healing benefits. I felt a hard "candy-like coating" building a wall around my throat and lungs. I had heard of many people being put on respirators and never coming off them alive. I thought to myself, *"Oh no! It is time for me to take this illness more seriously. I can feel how this hardness could be very dangerous."* I spent the whole night bathing in the love-light of the Divine. I imagined the Light shining on my chest, breaking the dark, hard, energetic blocks. When I woke in the morning, I was not 100% back to health, but I knew I had turned a corner in the direction of health, not the hospital.

I had another profound experience with light years ago during a tough emotional time. It was looking at another sleepless night because I was troubled by an event. My gut was clutching with anxiety due to an attachment I was being asked to release. My body was fighting what I knew my Spirit was calling me to do. I knew that this attachment was not part of my infinite nature. I decided I would permanently remove the painful attachment that night. My resolve was that I would stay up all night focusing on the area until it released. I put on some music with a repetitive drum beat and let my awareness circle around the area for hours as I drifted in and out of different states of consciousness.

About three and a half hours later, I finally felt a release from the emotional gripping. It felt like a "letting go," similar to how it would feel if you dropped something from your hand. Soon after that, I felt a flash of appreciation, and then an expansion into grace, and finally, I launched into beautiful Light with a moving tapestry of highly intricate, glorious imagery. It looked like those decorated walls in monasteries where there was not one empty space that was not filled with beauty. I was "on the other side," and I knew it. I removed the block that kept me from experiencing the Divine and lifted the veil between the worlds. I was on both sides; my physical body was in my bed, and my Spirit was awake in "heaven." I had cleansed the area enough to expand into a sweet state of consciousness that I can only describe with my limited vocabulary as exquisite, sweet appreciation.

I remained in this state for several days despite my external world reorganizing around a painful loss. To this day, I often relive this experience and marvel at how the excruciating emotional pain of an attachment inspired me to launch into luxurious Light! I followed the thread of releasing into good feelings, which led me to heaven. We all could do this if we were well disciplined.

Light has become such a constant companion in my life that if I don't know what to do in any situation, I rest in Light first. I may not understand what is happening, but I know I am moving the situation toward resolution. It may take a while for things to shift externally, but I am 100% confident that resting in Light helps it move along much faster and makes my life more enjoyable along the way. I would often return and find myself laughing loudly, demonstrating that my heart had experienced a healing. Light has a way of nourishing us and helping us have the energy to confront any challenges we are facing.

However, as much as I have had these experiences over the years, it was not until one situation that I acknowledged that Light is where I want to live at all times, especially as I face the unknown. I will not bore you with the details, but it was a project I had been working on for years. Things that should have been very simple were hitting roadblock after roadblock. The situation was both financially and organizationally costly. Finally, after several days, the simple/complicated situation was resolved, and I collapsed on the couch to assess the ridiculousness of what had just happened. I could not believe what I had endured for something so simple; it was a pattern I seemed powerless to overcome. I literally felt "beat up" in my energy field.

Then, down from the ceiling to my side, a column of purple Light descended. At first, I begrudgingly acknowledged the Light while raging at it, saying, *"You see what is happening! You are there; why must something so simple be so complicated? Why are you attempting to nourish me after I just got my ass kicked?"* The Light moved closer; I could feel it healing me. Eventually, I begrudgingly received the Light and allowed myself to be nurtured. I felt healed, whole, and at peace a little while later.

Soon after, I launched into three days of what I could only describe as "exquisite spaciousness." I can only assume this state was similar to what an opioid trip would be like. I would try to send an email, and then an enchanting spiritual intoxication would come over me. My eyes would roll back in my head, similar to how I have seen people who have just shot themselves with heroin are depicted in movies. I was definitely learning why I had heard of emaciated spiritual adherents sitting by the side of the road in India, often having to be fed and bathed because they were so entranced with the Divine they didn't care for their earthly bodies.

I still marvel at how light travels with me through trials. If I feel a stream of healing light entering my field, I have learned to acknowledge its presence by stopping and recognizing its wisdom, which transcends words. I will not even guess why this happens. I have no idea. Still, I have gleaned from these experiences that all of our suffering is observed from the other side, even if we don't feel it's support. I have learned that my ego mind may not understand, but I know I will feel stronger and renewed if I accept the grace that accompanies the Light.

Throughout the years, my love affair with light has deepened. For instance, I am currently in a phase where I often wake up with light shining from under my feet and upward. I feel the blessing of its presence, but I can be so dense because I still question its timing! I remember saying to Spirit one day, *"Really? Couldn't you have done this healing while I was asleep? I need to get up and accomplish things."* I guess I am a slow learner. I just never found this phenomenon that compelling; it was like, *"Yeah, and why are you here?"* I often daydream how much simpler my life would be without these experiences. Sometimes, I just want to play the "I am purely physical game" like most people do.

Living with Light makes you ask questions you would probably never ask without it. I can only assume that I am having more experiences now because of the years of cleaning of my energy field. Compared to when I began this work, my field now feels more integrous and beautiful. As messy as things got, resolutions kept leading to greater love and joy. I love feeling the frolicking of a light heart and living in a fun-freedom-loving state. I now see that situations and people who challenged me were merely pointers on recalling my Spirit to fix breaches in my Spirit's infrastructure. I finally came to accept that if I am working to change my energy field and feel happier, healed, and whole, it is a legitimate internal win for me, regardless of how things look externally.

I now drink drink daily from the wells of liquid-loving,

intelligent Light. My life is constantly changing course, albeit in delayed responses relative to my energy work, but I rest in the process now. I resist it less and employ it without questioning it all. I would not want to age any other way. The results are I have a lot of great friends, excellent health, make some money, and have good relationships with my kids, all while laughing a lot because my heart is light and my Spirit is untethered.

I would not go back for anything. I often say I am as happy as I am because of everything that went wrong. I can thank all my petty tyrant friends for that! LOL. Because of them, I learned the curriculum of releasing my attachments to harness my power. I apply these skills daily in all areas of my life. I am still tested with trials, as we all will be to our deaths, but this skill set holds me exceptionally well. My Spirit is more vital than ever. My internal energy gives me the confidence to greet the great unknown, including death, with excitement and awe. I write this book hoping that after you remain attentive to your energy field, these skills will serve you daily as well.

The sooner you associate how differently you feel after performing these mind-body-spirit disciplines, the sooner you realize how much you have started to learn from being a student at the Heightened Consciousness Spiritual Law School. You are beginning to master the curriculum of being an energetically informed human. You are learning how to calibrate your energy field to be in a humbled, proper rela-tionship with the Divine by cleansing your field of energetic blocks so you can mingle with Infinite Love. The good news is that you can start to feel heightened consciousness even as you face some of your life's most formidable challenges.

In this final mind-body exploration, we will continue

fortifying the skills we have cultivated and cleanse the energy field around our body, commonly referred to as our aura or biofield. We will review our lives, find areas that distort our field, and then practice releasing our attachments and infusing the area with Light. This is a skill I use daily. It sets up my day to accept my challenges as the up-leveling opportunities they are. I now live in wonder as I greet each day, not knowing how it will proceed but looking forward to all experiences as an opportunity to heal and merge with something greater than myself. I have accepted the spiritual curriculum of being a human on earth who is clearing karma so I can snuggle up and rest in the arms of Divine love. Life is quite simple when we become familiar with the spiritual curriculum in which we are already enrolled.

In the mind-body exploration for this chapter, I will encourage you to move toward a oneness state, which Taoism refers to as "heaven's viewpoint" where there are "no distinctions." To help us understand "heaven's viewpoint," we need to consider the viewpoint of Infinite Source Energy. If this Source Energy makes up everything, then there is nowhere that Source isn't, so everything is equal. Nothing is more important than anything else. No one is more important than anyone else. We will soften all the "hard" things in our lives and learn to feel softness everywhere, especially in our challenges.

You may not be ready for this consciousness truth, but the Divine is everywhere, just as I saw it in all the earth-bound technical difficulties at the EEG training. Remember, I saw the "perfection" in all of the technical problems. During the day, the technical difficulties were highly disruptive, yet the same difficulties were Divinely ordained in the other state of consciousness I experienced that night. Your linear mind won't want to accept this. There is no way to reconcile the darkness in this world other than releasing your regular nervous system filters to experience a nonordinary state change. You may not want to accept this, but the Divine is in your agony, pain, and petty tyrant. However, a higher part of you is in on the game.

We can't experience heightened consciousness until we learn not to recoil from our lives. I admit, people in the physical world can be horrible humans. However, we will practice infusing them with light, as it enables us to acknowledge that "God is in the details" without getting lost in our temporal pain.

If we want to *feel* heightened consciousness, the key to experiencing it is just that---to *feel*! But we are lousy "feelers." For the most part, we don't like to feel unless it is a positive state, but many of us even resist feeling good! To cleanse our fields enough to feel fabulous, we need to be able to feel our pain, which we eventually learn is caused by our recoiling from the Divine. As we feel into the pain of attachments, we bring light to heal them. We intend to have our dense burdens lifted from our energy fields, have them cleaned by Source Energy, and then have the energy returned to us as Infinite Love. In the mind-body exploration for this chapter, we will practice how to "God bathe" to transduce our burdens into love and then receive this love back to ourselves.

There is much more to this Light business, but I will leave that for future books. Until then, I would love to hear from you about any Light discoveries you make, as I am confident that you will have them if you keep practicing. There is so much consciousness to explore! Don't take this work too seriously and have fun with it!

After practicing the mind-body exploration for this chapter, I suggest repeating the meditations in sequence to see how they all fit together to fortify your integrity and worth. Notice how your energy field has already changed. How have you already stopped hemorrhaging your power?

I hope you have enjoyed finding new spaces in yourself through the skills offered in this book. I have pursued this approach for over thirty years, and it has held me very well. I fall more in love with life every day. I laugh easily and feel fabulous during mundane experiences like walking into grocery stores or putting gas in my car. Yet, if I were to leave this world tomorrow, I would be complete because I know where I am going. I am going where I practice living now as I experience a little heaven while still here on earth. I hope you develop a lifelong, enduring relationship with Light.

The mind-body exploration for this chapter is really just an entry point. Get creative. Light up everything in your life! Light up your petty tyrant, old disturbing memories, and current troubling situations. Become intolerant of being miserable by pre-paving everything with Light, intending for the most peaceful outcome for all involved. Most of all, light up your heart so you can smile! We will set an intention to have these burdensome densities lifted from your field, then cleaned and purified, and finally returning back to you so that you can use the refined energy to finance your life.

I strived to offer you some powerful skills in this book. However, this work is best taught in groups so we can share our experiences. The rich questions that arise among group dynamics help us all learn the material better and comprehend how the Divine interacts with us all. To that end, I am creating an online community to meet regularly to continue exploring cleansing our energy fields. As we gain reinforcement from others and hear each others' stories, it inspires us to stay the course during our darker, more uncertain times.

I did not have such a community, but I was fortunate to have had a heightened energetic awareness. I am certain I would have curled up in a ball a long time ago if I hadn't had this uncanny ability to know where my awareness was parked and how it could be profoundly directed to improve my life. I realize most people don't have that level of under-standing...*yet*! My work is to teach people how to focus their locus of awareness for more remarkable outcomes, espe-cially through our city-wide peace meditation research studies.

There is nothing special about me; I think Infinite Love showers all of us with Light, especially in our darkest times. We just don't know it! We learn this process to help us receive support from the other side and build the resilience needed to navigate this world. Then, our challenges can finally be utilized to facilitate the enjoyable magical mystery tour our lives were supposed to be. It is my sincerest deepest hope that I helped facilitate this process for you.

This mind-body exploration is just an entry point. Get creative. Light up everything in your life. Release any tension around both good and bad things. Even positive things can trap our energy. Release them as well to enjoy them more. Stay Sovereign. Over time, feel the difference as your body sinks into release, your heart lightens, and your energy field expands. You know the pathway now; detach your energy from adversity and reinsert it into yourself... Repeat through challenges. Enjoy strengthening your energy field a little more each day as you practice expanding into the delicious freedom of heightened consciousness.

You can find the mind-body exploration audio,
Releasing Our Attachments with Nourishing LoveLight at
NuminousOnline.org/pearl
Enter the password: pearl

© Bethany Gonyea 2024. All rights reserved

AN INVITATION

If you want to continue gaining the benefits of pursuing the *Consciousness Athlete* work in a more structured approach, I am creating several opportunities to continue learning within a formal Consciousness Athlete curriculum. Periodically, I will offer four-month Consciousness Athlete programs. Having studied with some of the most iconic healers of our time in the States and abroad, I have assembled this program by cherry-picking the best practices I have gathered over 30 years. You have experienced a sample of such content in this book. There is so much ground to cover. The journey to expanding consciousness is vast and could feel overwhelming, but I make each step manageable, offering specific feedback to help accelerate your results. I confidently teach with the secured end goal in mind because I want to inspire you that you are worthy of your own attention. You got this! Throughout this work, you will better understand the benefits of living life as a Consciousness Athlete.

As I've emphasized repeatedly in this book, your end

goal is to athletically conditioning your nervous system for heightened consciousness. There are two aspects of the live curriculum that I can not add to this book. These elements can dramatically accelerate your trajectory when integrated into your journey.

First, in the four-month program, you have opportunities to share your personal goals while receiving skilled, intentional coaching from the rest of the Consciousness Athlete class and me. Take that in for a moment. It is a unique and incredibly rare opportunity. For each class, you can enter your name and intentional goals on the master spreadsheet, so you will receive support to achieve your goals from fellow trained students' powerful, skilled intentions!

As we have learned, research demonstrates that intention has a "training effect." It is best to receive intentions from people who are trained. Since intentions are powerful, you want to be sure people sending intentions your way are sending them correctly! You will be confident that your fellow students will "have your back!" My students often joke that they know when it is their day to receive intentions because they can feel the "ju ju," or juicy energy, of the increased energy flow in their lives that day. That increase in power is often just what they need to "fall up" into a new state of being.

The second powerful aspect of this approach, one you will not see offered in many programs, is that I allow time for group communication. The wisdom from the participants, who have been cleansing their consciousness, is often appropriately insightful, revealing greater understanding for all of us. You may meet some of your newest, closest friends in our classes! We consider our time together a rare and precious gift. A student once expressed the importance of our class time together, saying, "*Frank and I could not make it to class... and we were truly pained by that.*"

Also, I am compiling a meditation library that will be a cornerstone of the website, offering an array of meditations created to meet Consciousness Athletes' advanced skills. These meditations are designed to guide you into greater physical mastery of your nervous system while simultaneously cleaning and expanding your subtle energy field. Each mind-body exploration is purposely created to help you successfully implement intentional skills in your daily life.

Additionally, most meditations include a set time for sending intentions to your life and to the lives of people you care about and love. This bank of meditations will be available for a small monthly fee. It will provide you with the daily training and encouragement needed to keep conditioning yourself to sustain lifted states of consciousness. Eventually, it will come with other perks as well, such as monthly webinars, etc.

Of course, you are always invited to participate in our city-wide meditations for no charge. We could use your help, *wherever* they are focused. There is no such thing as distance in the cosmic energy field. Connecting to others in the field of larger consciousness with a unified, focused intent for peace generates harmony and happiness in our lives. It is the best expansion fix of your energy field that I know! It reminds us that there is a bigger story that we are all living, and we can commune with loving energy to improve *all* of our lives.

Please stay in touch: **NuminousOnline.org**

© Bethany Gonyea 2024. All rights reserved